This book is a collection of radio monologues (*Dave's Raves*) written and performed daily over many years by Chicago news personality Dave McBride; a mix of witty wordplay, topical satire and observational humor.

"If you…haven't even heard of Dave McBride, all you need to know is this: The cleverest, most information-packed three minutes of radio in Chicago happens…when McBride, mild mannered journeyman broadcaster, is given an open mike and a license to rant, er, rave."—Chicago Sun-Times.

"… a tightly-scripted string of pop-culture observations and parenthetical asides … a densely packed combination of obscure historical references and goofball tabloid stories; sentences so long and convoluted a whole flock of nuns could spend an hour diagramming just one."—Chicago Tribune

"Best Three Minutes on Chicago Radio… a verbose symphony of rambling non sequiturs, odd lexicography, random quotes and freakishly obtuse vocabulary, plus some bizarre science and history facts thrown in for good measure. While the results are only occasionally intelligible, they're almost always fabulously entertaining."—Newcity

"Veteran newsman Dave McBride is perhaps the funniest man in the world—After an hour of reading you'll start to think in run-on sentences, but you're guaranteed quite a few laughs, too."—Daily Herald

The Book of Raves

An Anthology of Whimsical Monologues
63,683 words arranged variously

Dave McBride

The Book of Raves is a work of humor commentary. Some of the content exists only in the imagination of the author. Some is factual as reported in contemporaneous news accounts. These essays were written and performed daily over years as a satirical commentary upon current events and about random items of interest to the author. For purposes of time compression and creating an entertaining narrative, there contains some embellishment. While most subject matter in these pieces may be considered to be true, it may not be entirely factual.

Copyright © 2021 by Dave McBride

987654321 First Edition

All rights reserved. No part of this book may be reproduced, distributed, or transmitted in any form or by any means, including photocopying, recording, or other electronic or mechanical methods, without the prior written permission of the publisher, except in the case of brief quotations in a book review. For permission requests connect with the author at the web address below.

Library of Congress 2021906498

ISBN 978-1-7365138-0-4
EAN 51248
ISBN 978-1-7365138-1-1 (ebook)

Palapa Press
Boynton Beach, Florida

www.davemcbride.com

*To my Bonita Anita,
currently serving a life term as my cellmate
with no prospect of commutation to time served.*

The Book of Raves

Chapter 1—Next of Kin

How to be Happy

My great-grandfather, John Knox Montgomery, lectured on the Chautauqua speaking circuit at the turn of the century, when America's entertainment choices were limited to orators, banjos, and public hangings. And I still have a flyer advertising his appearance at Boulevard Hall in Chicago at Garfield Boulevard and Halsted Street on the evening of June sixth, 1902, when he delivered his trademark lecture entitled, "The Philosophy of Happiness." J. Knox would travel the Midwest explaining happiness to America's heartland. His advance posters read, "How to be Happy. That's what you want to know. That's what we want you to know. That's what the lecturer will tell you. That's what he will make you while he tells you." And from a press clipping of the time: "J. Knox Montgomery has few superiors as a public speaker. His lecture, *The*

Philosophy of Happiness, was heard by a crowded house last night. The audience swung from laughter to tears at the speaker's will." And the Chester, Illinois Clarion, wrote: "…a splendid address, full of truth, wit and eloquence."

And it has always been a source of lamentation in my family that the secret of happiness was once our birthright, but was lost. The story goes that, after his Chicago lecture, his bags were stolen from a train platform, and the text of the speech was lost forever, and he busied himself with other work and never reconstructed it. And so, from the time it was lost by my great-grandfather in 1902, the secret of happiness has been an elusive will-o'-the-wisp, an illusory phantasm, a chimerical unrealized dream. Until now.

A professor at Oxford University in England claims to have rediscovered the secret of happiness following eleven years of research. There are many things which are conducive to a state of happiness, such as chicken and dumplings and coming across, on late-night cable, the 1964 movie *The Moon-Spinners* where Hayley Mills becomes enmeshed in intrigue on Crete wearing very tight pink toreador pants. But Oxford professor Michael Argyle declares that the key, common to the majority of people who are happiest, is to have one close relationship, and a network of friends. One's income has no effect on happiness, except for the very poor, and having adulterous affairs make people less happy, because, while one close relationship makes for happiness, having two generally does not. Professor Argyle says people who watch soap operas gain a great deal of happiness from them, concluding that viewers acquire an imaginary close circle of acquaintances in this manner. The same could be said for listening to radio personalities with whom one comes to form attachments. Professor Argyle concludes people today are no happier today than they were a hundred years ago, likely because that was precisely when the secret of happiness was stolen from a Chicago train platform.

Meanwhile, California happiness researchers, working independently, asked college students from the Midwest and California which region had happier students, and while all were unanimous that California students must be happier, subsequent research found Midwest students equally happy, revealing that climate plays no role in happiness, unless one lives in a refrigerator box in Green Bay.

And although Professor Argyle says follow-up studies are necessary to confirm his formula for happiness, it seems as credible as a variety of previous theories. 19th century French novelist Gustave Flaubert was of the opinion that, quoting: "To be stupid, selfish, and have good health are three requirements for happiness, though if stupidity is lacking, all is lost." And it was Albert Schwietzer who wrote that "Happiness is nothing more than good health and a bad memory." And it was Ingrid Bergman who said that "Happiness is good health and a bad memory," happily having possessed a memory bad enough so as to have forgotten Albert Schweitzer already said it. And the great lesbian writer Rita Mae Brown concurs, writing: "One of the keys to happiness is a bad memory." And Rita Mae Brown has always been a definer of life's fundamental truths through the exercise of logic, for, as she once said, "If the world were a logical place, it would be the men who ride side-saddle."

Croquet

Napoleon called it, "the business of barbarians." Mao Tse-tung called it "politics with bloodshed," while the poet Byron characterized it as "the feast of vultures and the waste of life." My family calls it croquet.

I come from a family of primarily preachers and teachers and a more pacificistic and non-confrontational group of individuals it would be difficult to find outside a Mennonite barn raising. With the exception of when they are playing the game of croquet. The Montgomery side of the family (my mother's side), taciturn and reserved to the point of acetic stoicism at all other times, reverts to a primitive sanguinary ruthlessness, triggered (like a NORAD DEFCON alert to radar detection of inbound bogies) by the insertion of nine wickets and two posts into a lawn of short-cropped bluegrass. The grip of their fingers curled around the linen-wrapped grip atop a straight-grained shaft of ash attached to a brass-bound hardwood head with an inlaid sight-line, summons up a Mr. Hyde-like transformation; a feral brutish savagery which creeps upon them, like when Bill Bixby's eyes would turn greenish-yellow just before he transformed into the Hulk. My Uncle Paul, a mild-mannered Presbyterian minister, was unfulfilled in croquet until he could leave suffering and desolation in his wake like Sherman marching to Atlanta. The wails of the soon to be dead were music to his ears. And croquet-belligerency is genetically encoded into the Montgomery bloodline. When one's ball strikes another (a roquet), one has the option of taking two shots from a mallet's head away, or to squander the first shot after the roquet, the "croquet," by whacking the opposing ball to oblivion. Uncle Paul never failed to eliminate with extreme prejudice. His malice was palpable. My sister, too, was infected with the fever of croquet bloodlust and I still recall the sunny summer afternoon when she launched her mallet with explosive rage in a trajectory toward my brother's head, missing it by a quarter-inch, hurled with the power and precision of the Hammer of Thor.

In some families, the game is ended when the first ball has completed the circuit through the sequence of wickets and has touched the home peg. In my family, the desire to win was married to an equally intense desire to cause others to lose, and the primary strategic objective of the conflict was to become, at long last, Poison. The one who is Poison is the ultimate assassin. He who is poison achieves the mystical status of terminator; a supernatural annihilator whose slightest touch is death. Of course, even the Gods of Olympus had their vulnerabilities, and one who is Poison must guard against contact with a wicket or a peg; contact which terminates the terminator. One who is Poison must consider pegs and wickets anti-matter.

Through youthful indoctrination, I, too, came to know the intoxicating bloodlust rapture of Poison pleasure in lining up an easy shot to send an adversary straight to purgatory. My father, poor unfortunate, was a frequent victim, for, through his innocent arteries, flowed no Montgomery blood. I still experience the primordial pull of the mallet, and the urge to feel firmly beneath my foot the black ball, hard up against the red, and, with a smart whack, to propel my enemy out of the battlefield and into the Dyckman's back yard near the

Beagle kennel, resulting in much barking and general consternation.

And despite the return to dust of many Montgomerys, foreordained by Calvinist predestination; to this day, the brutality continues. At the Presbyterian Home where my mother resides, her apartment window overlooks a vast green lawn surrounded by towering trees they call the Meadows. Through this window, she plans her next scorched-earth aggression, each summer Saturday, at 9:30am, upon the field of Armageddon. Two knee replacements and osteoporosis have only served to make her meaner and more deadly when the war-wickets are at hand. And the day will come when the gods and goddesses of war update their regimental roster of those whose names are legend on the bloody killing ground, and uppermost, one will find my mother's name; Marge, warrior princess, mistress of the lawn between the pegs.

A Nail in the Head

I have to tell you what happened to me yesterday. And you know this isn't for the squeamish. Because for sure it gives me the heebie-jeebies and the screaming meemies and the jimjams and the wimwams and the willies. And there's no other way to say it, but; I had a nail in my head yesterday. See, I was up on my roof deck having a cocktail and this carpenter next door was driving nails with a nail gun and it went off and the nail ricocheted and went right in the side of my head and stuck there. A four-inch nail. See? I've got it right in this plastic cup (Shakes cup). So anyway, I felt this thing hit me right in the side of my head. In the left temple right behind the eyes. And I put my drink down and turn to my wife and say, "Say, honey. Does there happen to be a nail sticking out of my head?" To which she allows as how, yes, that appears to be the case. And she says don't touch it because you know how in the movies if you get an Apache arrow in you, you leave it in till the doctor comes because if you yank it out you bleed to death and the only good way to get the arrow out is to push it all the way through till it comes out the other side, which I hoped would not be the case with this nail, if you are with me on this. So she pulls the car around and on my way downstairs I can't help but peek in the bathroom mirror because it's maybe once in your life you can see yourself with a galvanized nail protruding from the side of your skull. Maybe twice.

So we go to the emergency room and for the first time in my whole life of emergency rooms, they don't ask me to fill out anything. No, instead they say, "You have a nail sticking out of your head. Come right this way." And you know they are pretty jaded in emergency rooms, having seen it all. But apparently they hadn't seen this. And it perked them right up; really brightened their dispositions. The main doctor appeared genuinely interested in me as a person with a nail sticking out of his head, and expressed the opinion that it was really quite a good big nail. So he pulled it out and put it in this cup and sent me to X-ray where the X-ray man was really very curious to see how far the hole went into my head. And as it turned out, it didn't go very far in at all which is something I will neglect to tell my wife because I figure I can get a heck of a lot of mileage out of this in the "bring me a beer and the remote control" department, if you catch my meaning. See, you probably know this, but wives always say men are such whiners; they don't much feel sorry for us when we get the flu or some such. But even the hardest of women will admit getting a four-inch nail shot into your head merits a little sympathy. So it's a happy ending: I get the pipe and slippers treatment from my wife. I get the nail out of my head. And a Lexus out of the carpenter.

Jew Cattle Buyers and Gollywobbles

It was while reading my grandmother's diary, just before the entry about hosting the Jew cattle buyers, that I came to question the absolute authority of the medical establishment in matters of what's good for us.

Microbiologist Stuart Levy at Tufts University in Boston says it's time to declare a moratorium on the slaughter of bacteria, in that we require infection to be healthy. The argument debated at a meeting on infectious disease in Atlanta is that not only does taking too many antibiotics lead to drug-resistant super-bugs, but that causing our environment to be sterile prevents our immune systems from the rigorous workout they require to develop resistance to infection. Dr. Levy recommends throwing out the antibacterial soaps and cleansers and the companies which make the anti-bacterial soaps and cleansers believe Dr. Levy is full of hooey, and Proctor and Gamble's statement is, "If you look at the way we live today, vs. the way we lived 50 years ago, personal hygiene has been a major contributor to improved health," and should they need supporting material I will refer them to the daily diary of my maternal grandmother, Anna Mary Thompson Montgomery, wife of pastor Don (Alonzo) Patton Montgomery, with which I was recently gifted.

She wrote an entry a day as a newly-mom newlywed farm-bred girl in her twenties in the twenties. Let's begin with Thursday, October 18, 1923: "Find skunk under back porch. Elsie died this morning. Funeral services at chapel." November 1: "Baby has terrible cold. I spend day doctoring it." November 2: "I go to Missionary meeting at Mrs. Wick's. Get sick there. Don brings me home. Dr. comes. Acute gastritis." November 7: "Still sick. Julbrie Barnes brings 2 rabbits and a squirrel. Don eats squirrel. I eat two raw eggs." November 11: "Feel awful. Take morphine tablet." November 16: "Get my stomach pumped."

1924 starts out no better. Sunday January 6, 1924: "10 below zero. Baby and I both have colds. Don has to get Ed Riel to start his car. Earl Gibson dies." Monday the 7th: "I have a beastly cold. Mr. Hogg died on the Sabbath." Then the Jew cattle buyers arrive and depart and on February 9 she writes: "Mr. Vincent dies. Have gas in my stomach." February 17: Don calls on Mrs. McKisson. She has the erysipelas." And, as erysipelas is a malady unknown to me, I consulted my Dictionary of American Regional English to discover that it is a catchall for any disease unidentified by medicine. The etymologists offer an 1871 entry in the Hoosier Schoolmaster, quoting, "And for erysipelas, I don't know nothin' so good as the blood of a black hen," unquote.

Returning to my grandmother's journal, February 18: "Baby has an awful dose of excema." February 23: "Stillwagon's call about their baby's funeral. I have a beastly cold." The 24th: "Mr. Singman calls wanting his sick boy baptized." The 27th: I go to basketball game in evening. Mercer girls win. Jonathan Snyder dies."

March 1: "I have collary morbus all morning." Which sends me back to the Regional English dictionary to discover Coleramorbus is also known as the gollywobbles or collywobbles, which is to say, stomach cramps and diarrhea. And that is five recorded deaths in seven weeks, in addition to colds, eczema, sick child baptism, stomach gas, erysipelas and the gollywobbles. The rest of the journal is packed with illness and rigor-mortised friends and neighbors stacked like cordwood and numberless entries such as "Killed and ate our first spring chicken. Sick to my stomach at night." Or, "Baby is better. Don is powerful sick at stomach." The only good news in three months was that the Mercer girls won, and it is not certain she was rooting for Mercer. Clearly, in Northwestern Pennsylvania in the early 1920s the operative axiom was, "Whatever doesn't kill you gives you the grippe."

I'll take the anti-bacterial soap, and if the Penicillin and Bi-cillin and Amoxicillin don't work anymore, that's why they invented Augmentin and Zithromax.

Anyhow, returning to the entry of February 1, 1923, in which grandma Montgomery writes, "I call on Mrs. Patterson and Mrs. Grassman. Have two Jew cattle buyers for dinner." By which I am convinced she meant Jew in the nicest possible way, in the manner of our Lord and Savior being a Jew and not referred to in scripture as Jewish, just it would not have occurred to Israelites to perceive of Goliath appearing a bit Phillistinish.

It is likely, when one is in the business of purchasing cattle for Kosher consumption, one's identity as a Jew is a matter of common knowledge within the livestock community, and it was demonstrably not my grandmother's intention to offend, in that she clearly hosted them for dinner, and was not an anti-Semite, although it could be supposed that, in that they were Jew cattle buyers in the vicinity on business, she may have picked a beef with them.

Buying a Car

My car is ready to turn over to 60 thousand miles. Which caused me to entertain the thought of trading in my Rav4, which is probably premature, in that this car has been nothing if not supportive and loyal to the McBride household for the intervening years since it attracted my attention at the dealership, as if to inquire of me, are you aware that "A Toyota," is a palindrome?

And I have grown close to my car in that it has never not found the time to take me where I wanted to go. If I wanted to go see The World's Largest Hockey Stick, it was never too busy. When, on impulse, I elected to take in a lecture on how dinosaurs are more like lizards than birds, it transported me there without complaint, perhaps feeling an affinity for dinosaurs in that it thrives on a diet of fossil fuel.

And I am always reluctant to shop for a new car because when one practices car haggling once every six years, one is no match for the professional automobile salesman who is a natural-born hornswoggler and bamboozler who can dipsy-doodle you right into a twenty-two thousand dollar demonstrator with eight thousand miles, no warrantee and full ashtrays. And whatever final deal I come away with, I can never shake my conviction that my dad could have gotten a better deal.

When the salesman pops the hood and directs me to "Look at this power plant," I might as well be observing an alien autopsy for all the organs I can identify. Whereas, when I was a boy, I recall going with my father to the used car lot and he would lift the hood of a Mercury Monterey or a Ford Galaxie and he would lean over and unscrew or unlatch the top of the air cleaner. It was the component which used to filter the air drawn into the carburetor, the apparatus which would atomize the gas and air to make the vapor suck-able into the vacuum created by the pistons and amenable to spark plug combustion until Detroit taught cars to self-inject like clients at the methadone clinic. And he would lift the air cleaner to his face and sniff it. He would sniff it and his face would acquire an expression of mild alarm, like a springbok detecting the scent of the hyena. Then he would unfasten the distributor cap, and take out the rotor, and sniff, that, too. He would sniff it with his eyes closed, as though it were the cork to a fine 1956 Alsace Gewürztraminer. Lastly, he would draw out the dipstick with a flourish, like Zorro unsheathing his blade, and he would bring it to his nose and sniff that, too. And the car salesmen would always react with surprise. It threw them off guard. After all, if used car salesmen were mechanics, they wouldn't be used car salesmen, and they couldn't be sure my dad did not know something they didn't; had acquired a nose for engine wear in some fashion and found the petroleum residue both nutty and insouciant. And giving the impression his olfactory examination had informed him of the quality and likely life-span of the vehicle, he would declare the value of the automobile, to which the salesman would acquiesce to his superior wisdom and the deal was sealed.

I, on the other hand, always feel as though, after I have driven away from the dealership, they draw the blinds and lock the showroom while the salesmen enjoy champagne and laugh themselves into exhaustion displaying my contract via an overhead projector to the amusement of all. So I am reluctant to get a new car, in that I really have no complaints about the one I have and am not eager to have to relearn setting the clock or the correct use of the valet key and overdrive button.

And whereas, in my youth, my prime car-buying imperative was that the Triumph Spitfire must be British Racing Green or nothing, I have now morphed into my father in that I am more concerned with side airbags than whether, with nitrous oxide injection, I could harness eleven hundred horsepower to do a quarter-mile in eight seconds. I will nod approvingly at a four cylinder rather than inquiring about the availability of a Holly four-barrel carburetor and competition cams with a solid rocker valve train and stepped headers feeding four into two into one collectors and Hirst linkage on a tranny powered by a 462 cubic inch big-block. It's enough to make one peer into the lighted makeup-mirror on the flip side of the visor and wonder when the James Dean of one's youth turned into Mr. Wilson.

Profanity Deficit Disorder

You likely saw the survey that sixty-one percent of Americans believe people in the USA are ruder now than a few years ago and that more than one third admit to using profanity in public, with a higher percentage of men admitting to foul mouth.

And this study was disturbing to me, in that it reminded me of my deficiency in this area of male behavior. With limited exceptions, I am congenitally and hereditarily unable to swear. When I was a boy I learned about bad words from Glen Orcutt, who was my elementary school's repository and final word on the whole lexicography of bad words.

But now that intellect instructs me that there is no intrinsic good or bad in words but only in the intent of their users, I still cannot comfortably cross into latrine-lingo-land even though the border crossings are now open. And I blame my father for my invective impotence. When my father was really boiling mad he would exclaim, "Great Crump." Otherwise, his customary expletive of choice was "Great Scott", or "Suffering cats!" While other dads were exclaiming, "Jesus H. Christ on a stick!" my dad would say, "Well, bless my soul." When Bill Mahoney's dad, who was among the best in the business, would GD and MF till we'd sidle away to avoid the lightning, my dad would exclaim, "Hail Columbia!" and "Jeez oh Pete!"

And when I was very young it bothered me, but as I grew older, I came to admire my father for being what he was, the Emperor of Euphemism. The Potentate of the Prudish Phrase. The Grand Vizier of Vapid Verbiage. Because, at its root it all means the same thing. Dang equals Damn. The meaning is exactly the same. The invective is identical. There is no softening of intent. It is merely swearing in another language, the same as if you smashed your finger in the car door and cried out in German, "Das dich gots leyden schend!"(God's passion roil you) Or, "Yeso Christo" which means a lot worse than just Jesus Christ in

Lithuanian. Or "Filho da puta!"(S.O.B aka M.F.) in Brazilian Portugese. Or the unpronounceable Turkish phrase which means "Son of a Donkey!"

Even when philologist intellectuals invented the fake language Esperanto, they knew swear words were essential, and so they made up "Fek!" which is the S-word as interjection. And they made up "putinfilac-o" for "son of a whore" and who says being a linguistic scientist isn't fun.

My inability to swear like a sailor in no way diminishes my admiration for those who can do it well. It is a requisite to language. Finley Peter Dunne wrote, "Twas intended as a compromise between runnin away an fightin. Befure it was invinted they was ony th two ways out iv an argymint." Of course, on the radio, it is actually helpful not to be blessed with a vulgar vocabulary. In the hallways we regularly hear the seven words George Carlin denoted as antithetic to a career in broadcasting, which are the s-word, the p-word, the f-word, the c-word, the c-s-compound word, the m-f-compound word, and tits. I know the words, but I am neurologically blocked from speaking them. Which is at the end of the day unsatisfying, because "Chuck you, Farley" is language decaffeinated.

Great profanity is an art form my family is genetically prohibited from mastering. Great profanity is like a well-crafted poem, or a movement in a symphony, wherein the notes join in a rising chorus toward a rousing crescendo. Great profanity can move the multitudes to awe and admiration. As Ralphie said of his father in *A Christmas Story*, "Some men worked in oils. My old man worked in obscenities." And the old man's creative genius in this area became abundantly clear when he was so angry no word in the English lexicon of profanity suited his mood and he coined the ultimate epithet, "NottaFinga".

So like Ralphie's father, and my own father, I continue to search for the perfect thundering fulminating malediction without actually using profanity. I use "mundanity," which one could describe as a well-crafted pseudo-swear. Like, "Up thine with turpentine, you gormless gunga hugger-mugger goofus-foozler heinie-hugging scum-sucking rotten ringtailed pansified ho-dad sad-apple poot-butt goobatron dipstick corn dog!"

Day of the Corner Cupboard

In 1836, old man McNary had the carpenters come and build him a huge corner cupboard in his farmhouse in Washington, Pennsylvania. In 1966, the State of Pennsylvania passed an act which resulted in that corner cupboard appearing in my bedroom last week. Old man McNary had a daughter, and her daughter turned out to be my mother's mother. Her brother Roy, my mother's uncle, inherited the farm in Pennsylvania, which is where my mother and father would dump us kids when they wanted to go do what healthy young adults who are in love do when they wish to pretend their vitality is not being sucked dry by egocentric preteen ingrates.

This farm is the location of the infamous "Sheep's' tails incident," notorious in my family annals, in which I collected several dozen sheep's' tails discarded in the barn after a recent shearing, and stacked them in the back of my father's station wagon, unaware that the heat of the day, in an enclosed car, would cause the millions of maggots inhabiting the sheep's' tails, to seek the shade of every nook and cranny of the vehicle.

And it was in the farmhouse that the corner cupboard resided, containing Aunt Rhoda's canned goods; eight feet tall, four feet wide, polished by one hundred thirty years of McNarys and Thompsons, until the State of Pennsylvania passed an act taking Uncle Roy's farm, under eminent domain, for a state park. They intended to dam the valley and let it fill up with water to make a giant lake for fishing and recreation, and so they auctioned off the tractors and the feed corn grinders and the fancy farmhouse banisters, and Uncle Roy moved to a retirement home and my mom got the corner cupboard, made from hand-hewn cherry wood.

And when my mom moved to a retirement home, the corner cupboard came to my house and the movers declared that this enormous piece of furniture had as much chance getting up the narrow townhouse staircase to my bedroom as the aircraft carrier U.S.S. Nimitz has getting into Lake Meade, and so they abandoned it in my garage. But it wasn't until my mother told me to give it up because there was no way that corner cupboard was going up the stairs, that I knew with a certainty that corner cupboard would go up the stairs, because defying one's parents is just as satisfying whether one is 9 or 79.

And so I began dismantling a portion of the cabinet and removed the elaborate heavy cornice and the eight foot boards on either side which tapered into the legs, and I yanked out ancient hand-forged wrought-iron square nails that had been hammered home the year Davy Crockett died at the Alamo, and was left with a piece that was a mere seven and a half feet long and three feet wide, weighing approximately two hundred pounds.

And so I ordered my son Jonathan to help me carry it inside and he declared it wouldn't fit, and I was not surprised that Jonathan would agree with his grandmother because it is well known that the reason grandparents and grandchildren get along so well is that they have a common enemy. And the only way to get this enormous wooden wedge-shaped monolith up the stairs was to carry it in such an awkward manner as to test Dr. Ujiki's protective mesh, surgically implanted years ago to prevent my herniated intestines from lurching out like the clown head when the jack-in-the-box crank reaches the climax of Pop Goes the Weasel.

And I do recall that, at one point, negotiating the first landing, I was heard to screech, My Leg! My Leg! as I was crushed between the banister and the V-shaped edge of the monstrous cabinet. And Jonathan recalls that bad words escaped my lips, but of this I have no recollection. And we wrestled it up two flights of stairs and I reassembled it in the bedroom, in the house in which I have decided I will die, rather than have to move that corner cupboard again. If this corner cupboard had been left floating following the sinking of the Titanic, not only would Rose have been saved, but Jack, too, and the entire ship's band, and the pursers and the wireless operators. And none of them would have felt the least bit crowded.

Mr. and Mrs. Stock Footage

On the TV news they reported a study that shows there is a causal connection between smoking and hearing loss, in which the people who were studied all live in Beaver Dam, Wisconsin. And it turns out that the researchers at the University of Wisconsin Medical School are forever studying the Beaver Dam-ians, who live southwest of Fond du Lac just past Horicon Marsh, the largest freshwater cattail marsh in the world. And the last time the scientists studied the smokers of Beaver Dam they concluded smoking can impair eyesight.

And I called up to Beaver Dam and spoke to Bev at Rhode's Wooden Wheel Restaurant on Madison Street, who says that, rather than being seen as medical research guinea pigs, the locals would prefer that, when outsiders think of Beaver Dam, they think of it as home to Herter's Duck Decoys. And so I called Herter's and spoke with Carol who told me the Magnum decoys are bigger than actual ducks and are easier for the flying ducks to see from high up, but the Styrofoam decoys have moveable heads so the flying ducks don't become suspicious of a flock of ducks on the water below all looking straight ahead, and because they are Styrofoam, if they are in the line of fire, a few shotgun pellets won't sink them. And she says another attraction she wishes people would think of when they think of Beaver Dam is Nancy's Notions on Beichl Street, because Nancy was the actual Nancy of Public Television's *Sewing with Nancy* (consult your local listings).

And I empathize with the citizens of Beaver Dam, because, once the media has identified one as an example of something, one may as well have the label tattooed on one's forehead, and, to the media, Beaver Dam will forever be that hearing-impaired smoking town with bad eyesight. But of course TV stations across America did not actually send crews to Beaver

Dam to film smokers, because they all maintain huge collections of stereotypes, on hand, which they call stock footage.

And both my wife and I have existed as stock footage at one time or another. In 1990, I was "Overweight Man on Stairmaster" for a story on the local NBC affiliate. They filmed me at my Health Club. And for months thereafter, when a story was about the effect of exercise on longevity, there would I appear, legs pumping away. The irony is, it was one of two times I have ever touched a Stairmaster. I have cross-country skied the equivalent of half the circumference of the Earth on the Nordic machines, but I have never been stock footage "Overweight Nordic Track Man"; only "Overweight Stairmaster Man."

In the mid-80s, Anita and her girlfriend Susan were socializing at a bar, when a TV crew filmed them smoking for a piece about some medical finding about women who smoke. And for a decade afterwards, long after she had given up cigarettes, whenever the TV news would do a story about women who smoke, there would be Anita at the bar. And when the story was about smoking in general, there would be a montage of smokers, including Anita at the bar. And they finally retired Anita at the bar when the *Scarecrow and Mrs. King*-Kate Jackson hair and the thick plastic glasses and the Peter Pan collar became a stock footage giveaway. But during her tenure as "Stock Footage Smoking Woman", the local station aired it often enough that she would be recognized in public. And, in fact, Anita's mother learned that her daughter smoked from seeing her on TV.

And as a result of this story about the Beaver Dam smokers, you can bet some local man's answering machine contained the message, "Hey Chet! Saw you smoking again on the news! I'll speak up so you can *hear* this." We who briefly achieve stock footage fame are happy to relinquish it. I gratefully abdicated my title, as did my wife, because generally, when one appears over and over in stock footage, one's image comes to symbolize something distasteful or sordid or unsavory or dreadful, to serve as a warning to others. Ask little Miss Napalm or Mr. Agony of Defeat. And for me the most interesting intelligence I take away from this days' research is that there are people living among us who own Styrofoam ducks with moveable heads.

A Death in the Family

An official period of mourning is underway at my house. I arrived home last night to be informed by my grieving wife and son about the sudden and unexpected passing of Avery, who worked for our family for many years in the position of pet bird. Avery McBride; Parakeet-American. To his friends, he was just Avery. He was just a blue parakeet, but he was a good bird, and into the afterlife, he already carries his own wings. And one could plainly see, long before the scientists announced that the theory that birds evolved from dinosaurs was inconclusive, that Avery didn't have a drop of Tyrannosaurus blood in him, because he was the most gutless of birds. I swear, every time we cleaned out his cage, for years, he thought we were going to eat him. And if you were on the couch all the way on the other side of the room and you'd raise your arm to stretch, he'd flinch. Actually, flinching was pretty much all he could do. He was untrainable. Friends would come over and say, "What can he do," and I'd say, "Well, I trained him to flinch -- watch this!" And I'd raise my wrist to look at my watch and he'd fall off his perch.

A few Christmases ago, Jonathan gave Anita one of those bird-call clocks, and never did Avery fail to chatter loudly in an effort to communicate with the northern oriole or the white-breasted nuthatch as they sounded the hour. Perhaps, in the evolutionary plan to grant birds the gift of flight, the tradeoff for aerodynamics was a brain the weight and size of a half a kernel of candy corn.

Happily, it turns out, for most purposes, a bird doesn't require a good head for thinking, and by way of example I offer the true case of Mike the Headless Chicken. In 1945, Farmer L.A. Olsen of Fruita, Colorado, held a young Wyandotte rooster to the chopping block and whacked off its head, following which Mike wobbled away from the block and resumed his routine scratching around the barnyard, stooping to peck as though he still had a head. Scientists later determined the head was chopped off high enough on the neck to preserve the brainstem intact, allowing Mike to continue to scamper around like a chicken with its head cut off. Farmer Olsen, out of curiosity, commenced to dropping grain and water down Mike's headless neck, and, but for his inability to crow, which he daily attempted to do in his gurgling way, Mike thrived for nearly a year and a half, and was pictured in Life magazine in October of 1945 posing next to his head, which Farmer Olsen kept in a jar of alcohol. And all who saw him wondered, upon viewing a bird which appeared in no way debilitated by the removal of his head with an axe; "What's a chicken have to do to get to the other side?"

Anyway, our family is no stranger to the death of domestic animals. I recall the many hours I spent behind the stove and under the clothes dryer with my boy's hamster, Festus, who defied lockdown time and time again as he tried ceaselessly to achieve his dream of one day getting inside a wall where he could decompose.

When Jonathan was younger, he went through so many hamsters that when we entered the pet shop, it was the hamster who drew the short straw that would have to come home with us. Hamster families on vacation would stop outside our house to read the historical marker describing the horrors that had occurred within.

But it was just yesterday morning that Avery was on his perch, happily engrossed in conversation with the bird in the mirror, as though he had not the germ of a thought inside his microscopic bird brain; and last night, there he was -- on his back on the cage floor with his little bitty claws in the air, his beak open wide in a silent scream. And, figuring that some powerful forces of nature, in the form of toxic tropical bird microbes, had to be at work here to knock off Avery with such dispatch, I tenderly picked him up, using a long pair of barbecue tongs, and I placed him in a tennis ball can. And I made one final medical check by shaking it up just to make sure he was as stiff and as hard as a croquet peg, and he was.

So this morning, as the wind-blown leaves swirled across the river near my house, I stood upon the bridge, as is our custom, and with solemnity, released my grip

on the tennis ball can and the plastic sarcophagus
slipped silently into the river and floated out of sight.
And I calculate that, depending on river traffic, Avery
ought to be drifting out into the Gulf of Mexico shortly
after the winter Solstice. My son Jonathan's only
reaction to the tragedy was in the form of a short
statement: "Are you kidding? I'm not touching that. It's
dead!"

Henry Ford Wanted My Chairs

I have a little personal family story to tell, about my
great-grandfather Thompson's chairs and Henry Ford.
Let me preface this story with some background. The
city of Detroit was founded in 1701 by Antoine Laumet
de La Mothe Cadillac, following his posting as
commandant of the fort at Mackinac, where, it is
rumored, he tired of being known as Cadillac of
Mackinac, and so declared that henceforth all must call
it Mackinaw, whereafter they began calling him the
Cadillaw of Mackinaw. Monsieur Cadillac established
the fur-trading outpost he liked to call the Paris of New
France, which he governed until 1710. The name he
gave it was Fort Ponchartrain du Detroit, which meant
Fort Ponchartrain "of the strait"; the strait being the river
connecting Lake Erie and Lake St. Clair. So when they
shortened the town's name to Detroit, its meaning
became, simply, "the strait" which means "connecting
river"; the name redundantly given the Detroit River,
which today means, literally, the "connecting river"
river.

Flash forward two hundred years. The Great Lakes and connecting river had brought industry to Detroit, and industry's chief captain was Henry Ford. And in the 1920s, when Mr. Ford was acquiring the Americana he was to assemble into the museum known as Greenfield Village, agents for Henry Ford showed up at my great-grandfather Thompson's farm in West Middletown, Pennsylvania, and told him Henry Ford wanted his porch chairs.

These were typical examples of early 19th century armless Windsor chairs of dark-stained cherry, which had resided on his porch, and, upon which, the farmhands would sit while removing their boots. These were everyday chairs, not at all out of the ordinary aside from the fact that they were coveted by Henry Ford. And it is not difficult to imagine my great-grandfather's inner monologue, reasoning with him furtively and energetically, employing an argument something along the line of, "If Henry Ford wants these chairs, and he is the most notable bloated plutocrat Mr. Moneybags who ever rode the gravy train to Eldorado (which was not yet then a Cadillac but rather the mythical kingdom of gold sought vainly by the Conquistadors), then I'll allow as how I'm of a mind to hold on to them." Because, up till that moment, they had been utilitarian and pedestrian articles of furniture. But after that moment, they were priceless collectibles never again to meet human boot nor buttock.

It's like the Antiques Road Show. Every week, people with heirlooms they have no intention of selling, present them for appraisal to be informed that if they were offered at auction, which they won't be, they would likely sell for ten thousand dollars, which they won't, because one would rather be able to show the neighbors their ten thousand dollar sideboard. My Windsor chairs, when they were new, didn't cost much. And now that they are old, and have, at long last, come down in the family to reside with me---over a period of nearly 180 years their per-year cost has amortized down to virtually zero, and they have become virtually worthless, which is to say, priceless. On the other hand, had my great-grandfather permitted Greenfield Village to acquire them, I would have to pay 12.50 per family member to see them. The distance from my house to Greenfield Village is two hundred seventy-eight miles and my Camry averages twenty-seven miles to the gallon highway, so a roundtrip would cost me twenty dollars and seventy-eight cents were I able to buy regular unleaded for ninety-nine cents. Not counting tolls and Taco Bell, it would cost upwards of sixty dollars to see them, had my great-grandfather Thompson sold those chairs to Henry Ford. Instead, I see them every day, which makes them worth sixty dollars times the one thousand, six hundred fifty-two days they have been in my possession; or ninety-nine thousand, one hundred twenty dollars. I figure I could easily swap them for a Cadillac, whose namesake was recalled from Detroit to France (The first recall of a Cadillac in Detroit history) and tossed into the Bastille following the death of his protector, Louis the 14th, who also had nice chairs.

Chapter 2—It's a Science

Time Flies Like an Arrow, Not a Boomerang.

Watching TV on the DVR can rumple the fabric of time, in the sense that, metaphysically, one's mechanism of locating one's self in time can be thrown out of gear. Last night I paused "UFOs, Then and Now," where thousands of Mexicans were videotaping flying objects in July of 1991, to take a phone call from my college boy, who argued the "pro" position on the question of parental disbursement of supplemental funds. And when I returned, I could see that, if I watched this UFO show to its conclusion, it would run past what would almost to a certainty be the start of a better show. So I jumped ahead to real time, and discovered I had surfaced, in this time-shift wormhole, into the midst of a commercial break. And without engaging a thought process, I attempted to fast forward through the commercials---which I could not do---because, even with the most sophisticated of recording devices, one cannot play a TV image which has yet to arrive at one's television.

We can't board the future until it arrives at the station. Which is one of nature's immutable laws. And why Nostradamus was a fake. There is no such thing as predicting the future because to see into the future means the future already exists, contravening the laws of physics which dictate that time has been, without variance, chronological since the Big Bang. There can be no argument that, in the case of the new camera you got for Christmas (which time-stamps your photos because you can't figure out how to switch it off), you cannot take a snap-shot of something that hasn't happened yet. Likewise, light reflected upon objects permits us to see them, and until the light reflects into our eyes, (time-stamping it the present), it cannot be seen.

Likewise, I cannot record the things which are spoken into this microphone and beamed at the speed of light into the broadcast ether, until I have spoken them; because, if I could, I could just stay home and just listen to myself.

If this were not true; if vision into the future were possible; it would mean the event has already been exposed to the light and is traveling backwards in time to surface into general view at the present. And should it be true that the present is merely where the already-accomplished future flows into the past, then we have no free will and we are, all of us, like an audio-animatronic Lincoln who may vary not a tick in word or gesture from the programming. If I, as an individual conversant with the works of Einstein only to the degree I have tasted his bagels, may be so bold as to explore one of his theories; relativity supposes that as one moves at near-light-speed, time for the traveler slows, relative to non-travelers, a postulate which has been offered as a method of time travel. But even so, the future greeting the traveler upon arrival will be one which has already arrived at its present, and the traveler would be a stranger from an ancient past, with no return ticket.

A poll last year found that 48% of Baby Boomers expressed an interest in time travel, while among younger generations, 58% would be very interested in traveling through time, likely to a time when they no longer have to abide Baby Boomers. The survey found a majority would like to be in Dallas when President Kennedy was assassinated or in the Holy Land during the life of Jesus, proving time travel will never be possible or it would already be recorded by history that Dealey Plaza was jammed from Houston Street to triple-underpass to grassy knoll with tourists from the future and that Jesus was blinded on the cross by the combined flashes of the disposable cameras of a legion of time-traveling looky-Lous stomping all over Golgotha taking selfies with the Centurians.

It has been said that time is what keeps everything from happening at once, but it could likewise be said that it is nature's way of preventing the attractive legal secretary sitting alone at the bar from knowing what you will look like in thirty years. Sure, it would be nice to know in advance into which elevator will step a dozen people getting off at floors below yours. But if the future already exists, then we are only players in a movie with our parts cast and our actions blocked on infinite history's soundstage and nothing we do can depart from a script for a cosmic Groundhog Day, now playing, over and over, in an infinite engagement in the theater of time. Which is silly, because, given that it took more than 12 billion years just to arrive at single-celled organisms, nobody is going to sit through that twice. Even immortals have better things to do with infinity. The only way to see into your own future is to pull up weather radar.

Insufficient Memory

The time is coming, say scientists, when it will be possible for the average Tom, Dick and Harry Q. Public to obtain all the information there is. Researchers at the School for Information Systems at the University of California at Berkeley say most of the world's data produced each year is being preserved digitally and will be made available on the Internet and that, when that day comes, everything everybody ever knew will be there for the knowing, although many of us will still prefer to watch the Great British Baking Show.

The study authors undertook to find out how much information there is, and then to figure out how much space we will need to store it. They divided up the means of storage into four.

Paper, of course, preserves information such as the Holy Bible and Sheb Wooley liner notes, which say that the singer/songwriter who had a number one hit with *One-eyed One Horned Flying Purple People Eater* was a cowboy actor who played drover Pete Nolan in *Rawhide* and in *High Noon* he was Ben Miller, the brother of killer Frank Miller and the first gunman plugged by Gary Cooper. He also wrote the theme song to *Hee Haw*.

Film preserves everything from the image of Oswald's Mannlicher Carcano, to the photographs of every Thanksgiving turkey I ever cooked.

Magnetic media stores the video of the performance of George Bernard Shaw's *Major Barbara* by the Ashtabula, Ohio, Community Players at the Falling Timbers Outdoor Amphitheater captured in its entirety by my cousin Phil on High-8 in 1993.

And optical devices can display such material as the DVD director's cut of *Porky's II, The Next Day*.

The west coast researchers generated the following information in their pursuit of information: In the world, more than 80 billion photographs are taken annually, including those in which the only distinguishable object is the wing of the airplane. Also, the number of movies produced every year is numbered at approximately 4,250, including some in which Idris Elba does not appear. In the study, the scientists assigned each piece of information a digital size measured in bytes; the average photo 5 megabytes, an X-ray 8 megabytes, a feature film 4,000 megabytes, and so forth. Then they added up all the space needed to store all the books and movies and CDs and radio and TV shows and newspapers and magazines and snapshots, and arrived at two exabytes, which is a billion-billion bytes; times two.

This information overload will likely not affect those of us who can't remember whether we need to write our middle initials when endorsing our paychecks, as our cerebral cortexes remain blessedly untrammeled by the incursion of intruding information. Whereas those whose cranial recesses are cluttered with the knowledge that Freddie Mercury was born Frederick Bulsara in Zanzibar and also recorded under the name Larry Lurex, face the very real danger, in the new information age, of their heads exploding. The good news is the study authors do not expect us to pay attention.

They say the total time American households spent reading, watching TV, using computers and listening to music in 1992 was 3,324 hours, and since then we have increased that time by only 56 additional hours per year. The world produces a billion billion bytes of information a year times two. Of that total, the average person is exposed to 3 million 344 thousand 783 megabytes. Or, put in the kind of visual terms we journalists enjoy employing (usually stacking things end-to-end to girdle the globe or reach the moon), we are exposed to enough information per year to occupy all the space on a sufficient number of 5 gigabyte hard drives to fill Yankee Stadium, of which we will actually remember little more than fragments of song lyrics and ingredients to the occasional rum drink.

And the Berkeley scientists say that, in the U.S. alone, 610 billion E-mails are generated every year, 600 billion of which are forwarded to me with the joke of the day, which today is the one where Bill drinks up at last-call and slides off the barstool and falls on the floor, and tries to get up but falls down again and he knows he had too much to drink but can't stay on his feet, and, after falling down a half-dozen times he decides to crawl home on his hands and knees and he crawls up the stairs to bed so as not to risk waking his wife by falling over, but the next morning his furious wife gives him the stink-eye and demands to know if he got drunk again last night and Bill is surprised at being busted as she was asleep when he got home and he asks "How did you know?" and his wife replies, "The bar called and you forgot your wheelchair again."

The Mother of All Mothers

The things science can do is remarkable, and I'm not just talking about the opportunity science has provided us to step outside on a February morning and complain that it's "colder than Ted Williams' corpse." But of course the increased complexity of technology increases the opportunity for human error, which is how a white British couple who paid for test-tube fertilization wound up with black twins.

The British High Court ordered the press to identify the Caucasian couple only as Mr. And Mrs. A, and their dark pigmented babies as YA and ZA. And Ya and Za were apparently issued boarding passes to the wrong birth canal gondolas. And the test tube baby experts say the mistake could have occurred in one of three ways, which would suggest that those three ways should probably appear on a zygote recipe checklist. If the wrong sperm was used, the father is black. If the wrong egg was used, the mother is black. If the wrong embryo was used, both the biological mother and father are black, although Mr. & Mrs. A make it clear they intend to raise Ya and Za as their own. They contend that Ya and Za grew into multi-celled organisms within the friendly confines of Mrs. A, and despite darker complexions than their mom and dad, the blood in their veins is as Caucasian as croquet. And despite Mrs. A having quite clearly carried the twins to term, a judge will decide to whom the babies belong and whether race is determined by skin or blood. The blood proponents certainly have been nit-picks throughout history, calculating to the fraction how many drops of co-mingled blood is required for one to be hanged as a Negro or to be considered a Jew for purposes of assigning one-way boxcar transit or to be entitled to monthly Wind River Shoshone Reservation oil well revenue payments from the Department of the Interior.

Interestingly, according to theoretical anthropologists, everybody used to be black, and those of us who aren't turned white fairly recently in Homo history. Theoretical anthropologists have it that whites became whiter and whiter moving north out of Africa and the reasons are three. Near the equator, where the first proto-human picked up a stick and bipedaled his way out of the trees and onto the Savannahs, ultra-violet rays from sunshine are brutal. Far north of the equator, the UV rays are weaker. UV rays cause the skin to produce folate, which is part of the B vitamin complex, and also vitamin D-3, both of which are necessary for producing healthy human embryos. Too much UV can damage folate. So black skin is black as a UV sun block to preserve folate for producing healthy babies, and white skin is white to suck up more UV rays to produce vitamin D to produce healthy babies. Others say white skin is white because it gave early Europeans camouflage protection in the snowy north. It has also been shown that white skin is more resistant to frostbite than black skin. It was Paul

Valery who said, "Man is only man at the surface. Remove the skin, dissect, and immediately you come to machinery." And it is clear as the visible man that if the skin be transparent, the viscera beneath, identical across race, is equally as icky.

And black babies born to a white mother is a tempest in a test tube, when one considers anthropological evidence that humankind's family tree is rooted in a common mother. In 1994 scientists announced the discovery of the fossilized remains of man's oldest ancestor, a three-foot crocodile, in Hyner, Pennsylvania, concluding that mankind originated in the Keystone State just off I-80 just west of Williamsport behind the Susquehanna Mini-Mall Cineplex. After that, scientists discovered fossilized evidence that the earliest amphibian who would, eons later, develop the ability to arrange hooks on pegboards, first waddled up onto the coast of Ireland, suggesting that everyone actually is Irish and not only on St. Patrick's Day. And now Dr. Daniel Gebo of Northwestern University traces mankind's earliest ancestor to a rock quarry west of Shanghai, where, more than forty-five million years ago, there was a teeny tiny monkey who lived with teeny tiny rhinoceroses in a teeny tiny geological epoch called the Middle-Eocene, forty million years before the first Homo erection.

So the newest conventional wisdom is that the mother-to-us-all was not from Olduvai Gorge in deepest Africa, nor the Keystone State, nor the Irish Isles, but, rather, was a teeny tiny primate with the metabolism of a hummingbird who was snack food for prehistoric owls.

Who was Chinese. And thus are we all. But don't call me oriental. I prefer Asian.

What Was the Name of Pavlov's Dog?

I have, for some time, been searching for an answer to the query posed in an E-mail, which asked whether I could put my hands on the answer to the question: What was the name of Pavlov's dog? When we speak of some knee jerk automatic reaction to some stimulus, we invoke the name of Ivan Petrovich Pavlov, the famous Russian psychologist who discovered the conditioned reflex and developed an artificial stimulus to induce salivation, a technique perfected by Victoria's Secret. And we know he employed a dog in his research, but what name did it answer to?

And we know that Johnny Quest's dog was Bandit, and *The Call of the Wild* dog was Buck, and Roy Rogers had Bullet, and that the farmer had a dog and Bingo was his name-o. And that Mr. Magoo thought he owned a dog named Bowser who was really a cat, and that Butch kept Tom away from Jerry, and Nipper was the one who listened to His Master's Voice on the Victrola, and Mrs. Dreisdale's poodle was Claude, and before Goofy was Goofy he was Dippy Dog. And on *Magnum*, Higgins's dogs were Zeus and Apollo. And that the name of the Greyhound on the *Simpson's* who was leading at the dog track was She's the Fastest, followed by Always Comes In Second, and I'm Number Three. And that, also in the Simpsons, it was the union of She's the Fastest and Santa's Little Helper who produced *2 Dozen and 1*

Greyhounds, including King, Queenie, Prince, and the Puppy formerly known as Prince.

And we know that the guy in the beagle suit on the Banana Splits was Fleagle and that Sergeant Preston owned King and that I once had a DC comics subscription to *Krypto the Superdog*. And that Dorothy had Toto and Tom Terrific had Mighty Manfred, and that there is a school of thought that Fred Basset wasn't worth the newsprint he's printed on and that goes double for Marmaduke. And also that there is a school of thought that Lassie was the all time smartest dog, although I believe it was Mr. Peabody. And we know that Fifi is a horrible name for a dog. And that when one thinks of *Underdog*, the theme song automatically starts playing in one's head. And that Laika the space dog was a stray picked off the streets of Moscow and selected by the Russian space program to become the first living creature to burn up in re-entry. And Clutch Cargo had Paddlefoot and the Little Rascals had Petey and Rusty had Rin Tin Tin. And the Taco Bell dog Dinky and Ren of Ren and Stimpy are both Chihuahuas although they look nothing alike. And Little Orphan Annie had Sandy, and Tramp mounted Lady and sired Scamp, and Scooby Doo's nephew Scrappy was possessed of far better enunciation, and George of the Jungle named his elephant Shep. And we know that those country yokels should have pronounced the name, "Old Yellow," and that the same Yellow lab who played *Old Yeller* starred in *A Dog of Flanders* two years later so he didn't really die. And that Dick and Jane would often pause in their daily activities to See Spot Run.

But nowhere in my research through voluminous reference material at the public library to the University of Illinois Internet site maintained by grad student Misha Lunchbox, who has compiled a huge collection of famous dogs, was I able to produce a certifiable, confirmable, name of a single salivating St. Petersburg lab dog, by which I don't mean Labrador but laboratory. Not until I spammed the entire Department of Psychology at the University of Chicago.

And Professor Joel Pokorny return-emailed an entry from Pavlov's "Selected Works," Foreign Languages Publishing House in Moscow, translation by S. Belsky, page 356, in which Pavlov refers to the responses of the dog, "Bek." And, so, at long last, we can say two things with certainty. One: Bek was a Pavlov dog. And two: Pavlov's Dog is a fine name for a rock band, judging from the number of them which already exist; and what would happen if the same venue booked Ivan Pavlov's Dogs; the Detroit band, and Pavlov's Dogs; the Oak Creek, Wisconsin Band, and Pavlov's Dog; the St. Louis band. It would be a rocking Pavlovian dogfight.

The Sex Life of the Rattlebox Moth

Scientists at Cornell University, in addition to knowing the original lyrics to *Far Above Cayuga's Waters*, the world's most plagiarized school song, whose most familiar part is where it goes, "Lift the chorus, Speed it onward, Shout it to the sky, Hail to thee our Alma Mater, Hail to (insert your school name here) High…" have announced having discovered conclusive evidence to bolster the theory that Nature Is A Freak Show.

This conclusion was reached following an exhaustive study of the rattlebox moth, a flamingo-pink and black & white insect found mainly in central Florida. And it turns out the female rattlebox moth is given lifelong protection from predatory spiders through chemicals in the male semen; the injection which immunizes, as it were. I spoke with Dr. Thomas Eisner, an entomologist who has been working at Cornell since 1958 and who has been working with rattlebox moths since the 1970s, and asked him if he had heard the one about the centipede who complained about starting the day off on the wrong foot, to which he replied in the affirmative.

And Dr. Eisner explained his findings, which are that the male rattlebox moth, while he is a caterpillar, eats exclusively from the rattlebox plant, which is a plant so named because when the wind blows the beans in their pods make a rattling noise. And there are chemicals in the rattlebox called pyrro-lizidine alkaloids. Then, when the male rattlebox moth has sex with the female, he transmits these chemicals into her and they cause her to forever taste bad to spiders. And I asked him, in my ignorance, whether this intercourse occurs when the insect is a caterpillar or a moth, to which Dr. Eisner responded patiently, in the way intelligent people speak to doofuses, with four words, which, in a half century on the planet, I have never before heard lined up in a row: "Caterpillars have no gonads." And he went on to say that after the male immunizes the female during mating, so vile does she taste to a spider that the spider will actually cut a captured female out of its web to release her. In clinical studies, spiders rejected a female moth thus injected after a single touch. And after a series of laboratory experiments, a documentary film voiceover reader might say, "Unknown to this male rattlebox moth caterpillar, we've switched his rattlebox beans with pinto beans; now, let's watch what happens." And what happened was that the female who had sex with a pinto bean male rather than a rattlebox bean male was placed with a spider and, to her surprise, was promptly eaten.

And I asked Dr. Eisner as to the significance of these moth-eaten findings to which he replied that at least it adds one more item to the short list of "What Are Males Good For?" displaying the characteristic entomological wit which created "Time flies like an arrow, but fruit flies like a banana."

Anyhow, Dr. Eisner continued to teach me in the ways of love of the Utetheisa Ornatrix, which fills up on food while a caterpillar, because, for the thirty days of life it enjoys as a moth, having sex is its solitary endeavor. Eisner says the male moth couples with the female in the usual way, with a protuberance resembling a penis, but the similarity to human intercourse ends there, in that the delivery of the moth semen, which includes nutrients as well as sperm, takes nine full hours, three times as long as it takes NASA to fill the three main engines of the space shuttle. This is $1/80^{th}$ of the male moth's entire life, or in terms of a human male living to the age of eighty, an ejaculation duration of one year, and he may repeat the performance several times. Displaying even more endurance is the female rattlebox, which will continue to mate with any male so inclined and may have sex twenty times within her lifetime, which, in terms of a human female living to the age of eighty, would amount to two full decades of nonstop intercourse. And the final fact about this act elevates the event to at least a pay-per-view, because it turns out this single delivery of sperm to the female by the male rattlebox moth weighs more than ten per cent of his entire body mass, or the equivalent in a man of producing enough sperm to fill a volume the size of his own head, which is the product of what, one will agree, are some monumental mothballs.

The Fact of the Matter

I was reading in Popular Science about how 550 physicists worldwide are out looking for anti-matter, because in the beginning there were scads of it but over a period of fifteen billion years it got misplaced. And NASA's Chandra X-Ray Observatory has been up in space for more than four years now, and in that you chipped in for the purchase price of one and a half billion dollars, plus around another billion and a half to operate it, you might be interested in what it does.

The Chandra X-Ray Observatory is looking for dark matter. For our purposes, matter may be defined as what you see with your eyes open. Dark matter is what you see blindfolded with your eyes closed on a moonless midnight in a windowless room. If you can't see it, it is dark matter. And by now we have become inured to scientists charging us billions of dollars to look for things we can't even see after they find them. We taxpayers say, "OK, whatever," and write a check because it beats having to sit through a physics lecture.

Anyway, the Chandra telescope can detect the presence of certain matter by sensing gamma rays. And gamma rays are what happens when a positron collides with an electron and produces energy, the recipe for which, if one cares to jot it down, is, E=MC squared. A positron is anti-matter, and we should backtrack just a bit and begin at the beginning. In the beginning, inside a trillionth of a second after the big bang, in a flash of heat of such incredible intensity as to create all the atoms which were ever created quicker than half a flap of a hummingbird's wing, the universe contained equal quantities of matter and anti-matter. Matter was made from atoms containing a nucleus surrounded by negatively charged electrons and positive-charged protons, while atoms of anti-matter contained positively charged electrons and negatively charged protons, which, to belabor the obvious, are the opposite.

And they say opposites attract, but if matter and anti-matter even so much as brush up against one another in the elevator, they destroy each other in a flash of energy and turn into gamma rays and at the instant of the big bang nearly all the matter and anti-matter destroyed each other faster than a quick-draw high-noon shootout on the streets of Dodge. But for some reason unknown to anybody, the matter destroyed more of the anti-matter than vice versa, leaving gobs of matter strewn about the universe, leading to the physics axiom which describes matter as "weird enough so that it does not get in the way of God's freedom to make it do what he pleases." And the Chandra X-Ray telescope detects the gamma rays produced by anti-matter annihilation, in that detectors of anti-matter itself already exist. You are an anti-matter detector. I am an anti-matter detector. Because, should we ever find ourselves in the same room with anti-matter, should we shake hands by way of introduction, we would vanish in a flash of cosmic combustion, by virtue of our having detected anti-matter. And this is part and parcel of the attempt by scientists to disclose the quantity in the universe of what is called, "dark matter." Because, if there is a huge amount of it, the mass of the universe might be great enough to stop the outward motion of the objects in the universe and pull them back to their origin like the rubber band on a red rubber paddleball. But if there is not a lot of it, the universe will keep expanding for a million forevers.

And so I called Fermilab and Dr. Stan Wojcicki told me the biggest question has been whether the abundant subatomic particles called neutrinos have mass, or weight. And to that end he is building a neutrino detector a half a mile deep in Minnesota's deepest iron mine up near the Canada border, and one day at Fermilab they will make neutrinos in their particle accelerator and shoot them right through the solid earth where they will pass through everything in their path underground and arrive 450 miles away in 4/10ths of one millisecond and when they get there, if they have transformed to another kind of neutrino, they will know that neutrinos have mass; and never mind that Canadian scientists have already proven that they do. And it occurred to me as I was speaking with Dr. Wojcicki that neutrinos would be a dandy name for a breakfast cereal.

And there will be some who will ask whether detecting anti-matter and dark matter will impact upon the daily lives of any of us in any measurable way, to which it, must be confessed, that the answer is no. But as the physicist Richard Feynman put it, "Physics is like sex: sure, it may produce some practical results, but that's not why we do it." And a NASA press release calls the search for dark matter the greatest of cosmology's unsolved mysteries, as separate from cosmetology's unsolved mysteries such as why it is necessary to rinse and repeat.

Out of My Periodic Element

It seems like only yesterday that the scientific press reported, with excited twitteration, the discovery of element 118 by physicists out west.

Like my pal Stumo, who shot beer cans off tree stumps to ascertain how a .44 caliber round-nose flat-point would physically alter their appearance, scientists are forever shooting particles of this or that at one thing or another and will, from time to time, examine the aftermath and have occasion to say, "Well, now lookee here," which was the case when, two summers ago, element 118 was spotted lurking around the Lawrence Berkeley National Lab. And Lawrence Berkeley Lab is not named after Lawrence Berkeley, but, rather, is in Berkeley and is named for Ernest Orlando Lawrence, who, in 1931, invented the Cyclotron, which everybody agreed was a dandy machine, but as it was the Great Depression, sales were sluggish. And it was there that scientists, firing up the 88-inch Cyclotron (which would be a fine name for a metal band), shot Krypton into lead, which had no effect in Superman Comics, but which, in this case, produced element 118, which, with a half-life measured in micro-seconds, decayed instantly into element 116, which then decayed into element 114.

Because in physics, as in life, one can often only detect what one has created by the remnants it leaves behind, such as a half-eaten hoagie on the kitchen counter or a 30 thousand dollar invoice for tuition, room and board. And it was quite a stroke of good fortune, given that people had been searching for element 118 all over the world for many years, that it happened to turn up in California, right in the exact spot where these scientists were looking for it. I was very fortunate to have gone to school at a time when a mere 105 elements resided on the Periodic Table and I still got a D on the chemistry final.

Element 118 filled up the 115th box on the Periodic Table with elements 115 and 117 remaining among the missing and undiscovered. Because it turns out that scientists don't just announce the introduction of element 105 and figure to name the next element they stumble over 106. The atomic numbers are arrived at by the number of protons in the element's nucleus. And, as you might imagine, the difficulty in identifying an element whose half-life is way shorter than a shadow cast by a Sylvania Blue-Dot flashbulb, would be hurrying to count up the protons all the way up to 117 faster than a quarter-flap of a hummingbird's wing.

Anyhow, this element 118 was in the family of elements characterized as super-heavy, and could one construct tableware out of this new element, it would be a good gag to watch dinner guests at the weight lifter's convention struggle to lift their forks to their mouths using utensils with an atomic weight equal to a ton in a teacup. However, it turns out that one will not be constructing salad forks from element 118, because, fact is; there is no element 118.

Imagine my consternation when scientists from Lawrence Berkeley Lab wrote into Physical Review Letters, which publishes notes from physicist pen-pals, to sheepishly confess it appears they didn't discover element 118 after all, after scientists from around the world protested that they hadn't been able to duplicate their results. Which certainly cries out for a class-action suit on behalf of anyone who got it wrong on the mid-term. Where is the justice for those who have been, for the past four semesters, compelled to memorize the element ununoctium, when there is no such thing? The justice, my friends, will derive from the derision from their peers, as physicists are world-class scoffers, and will soon be E-mailing one another with lines such as: How do you determine whether Lawrence Berkeley scientists are out of their element? You look at who's operating the Cyclotron and count up the number of morons.

Fruit Flies Like A Banana

18th century behaviorist and historian Nathaniel Wanley wrote that "The brain is so vigorous and active it insinuates itself into all places and times; reaches the heights, searches the depths, peers into all those recluded cabinets of nature wherein she hath stored up the choicer and abstrusest pieces of all her workmanship, and these, it contemplates and admires," which was recalled to me as I read the news that scientists in Japan have been growing frog's eyeballs in Petri dishes. And this is a happy continuation of the groundbreaking work of American scientists who have been growing fly eyeballs on the legs of fruit flies of the order Drosophila Melanogaster; work which will result ultimately in making high school biology way more fun.

In my school, Mr. Weiss was our science teacher because the basketball coach had to teach something, and it wasn't much fun except for what one could do with the ink sac after dissecting the squid. Although I did enjoy biology lab because my lab partner was Glen Orcutt, and when we examined our cut-open flatworms Mr. Weiss told us that it was a simple creature mainly consisting of gut and gonad, and Glen leaned over and said, what else do you need? And when teetotalling Mr. Weiss wished to demonstrate the evils of spirits and dropped one-after-another of the remaining flatworms into a beaker of water and a like number into a beaker of Ethyl Alcohol, and the ones in water wriggled happily while the flatworms in the alcohol shriveled and died, he queried, "From this, what may be extrapolated?" to which Glen Orcutt replied, "If you drink alcohol, you won't get worms." Which he didn't actually say and was an E-mail joke somebody sent me but I swear it's vintage Glen Orcutt.

Anyhow, Japanese scientists found out that if you take embryo cells from frogs and put them in a dish and cover them with a solution of retinoic acid, organs start to grow. And a lower concentration of retinoic acid causes frog eyeballs to grow, and a higher concentration causes frog ears to grow, and so they can grow as many frog eyes and ears as world demand cries out for. And they can also grow frog kidneys, which they have successfully implanted into frogs that lived for a month in people time, which is seven months in frog months. And they claim it is a step toward being able to grow human organs for transplant. But if you ask them "when?" they will hem and haw, and if you ask "will it be in ten years?" they will say, "Way past that," so the only earthly reason they continue to grow thousands of frog ears is because they like it and enjoy making their female associates come over to look at their big jar of frog eyeballs. Just like biologist Roger Sperry at Caltech wired the left optic nerve of a toad to its right brain and the right optic nerve to its left brain and when the toad tried to catch a fly coming in from the left its tongue would shoot out to the right and vice versa. Or molecular biologist Ed Lewis, also at Caltech, who made mutant fruit flies with legs sticking out of their heads instead of antennae. And the Caltech flyboys also made fruit flies with the right half male, and the left half female. Nothing beats Caltech fun with Drosophila.

Which reminds me of the part in "Through The Looking Glass," when Alice is going from square to square on the chessboard trying to find her way home and she has a discussion with a gnat the size of a chicken who asks her, quoting, "What sort of insects do you rejoice in, where YOU come from?" To which Alice replies, "I don't rejoice in insects at all…but I can tell you their names." And she allows as how she's never heard an insect answer to its name, but suspects insect names must be useful to the people who name them.

And the Japanese scientists growing frog ears recalls to mind the story where the scientist records in his log that, after prompting with a vocal outcry: "Jump, frog, jump," that a frog with four feet jumps 4 feet. Then he surgically removes one of the frog's feet to record that following his cry of "Jump, frog jump," a frog with 3 feet can jump but 3 feet. And removing another foot he notes that at his shout "Jump, frog, jump," the frog can now only leap 2 feet. At which point he cuts off the final two feet and cries again, "Jump frog jump," and notes in the log that a frog with no feet becomes deaf.

The Secret of Einstein's Brain

I was engrossed by the story of Dr. Ehud Arbit, at Staten Island University Hospital, who got in trouble accidentally operating on the wrong side of a woman's brain. For the patient the bad news was the surgery was performed on the opposite hemisphere from the abnormality. The good news was her memory of the experience was removed in the operation. And it occurs to me that Dr. Arbit is one of the relatively few Americans who can't shrug and say, "it's not like it's brain surgery."

One feels a disturbance in the force of one's belief system regarding intellect when a brain surgeon is a bonehead. It was said by 18th century physicist and satirist Georg Christoph Lichtenberg (who was so smart he discovered the principal of modern xerographic copying the year after the Declaration of Independence and 163 years before Chester Carlson would use the principle to invent the actual Xerox machine), that

"Sometimes men come by the name genius in the same way that certain insects come by the name centipede; not because they actually have a hundred feet, but because most people don't count above fourteen." In other words, geniuses shine only when included in a lineup with the rest of us dimbulbs.

Recently the Journal "Physics World," which reaches out and grabs the reader with article titles such as "The Underdoped Phase of Cuprate Superconductors," and "Silicon Germanium Makes Its Mark," took a poll of subscribers to compile a consensus of which were the top ten physicists who ever lived and number one is Albert Einstein, the relativist who once posted a notice that "The lecture on faster-than-light-speed will be held two weeks ago," and was said to have asked a conductor, "Pardon me, but does Baltimore stop by this train?"; whose theories helped develop atomic fission, without which there would be no Amazing Colossal Man. Should Einstein fail to fulfill the egghead obligations of the appointment, the first runner-up, who would recognize the gravity of the position, is Isaac Newton. Rounding out the top ten brains of physics are James Maxwell, whose equations described electromagnetism; quantum theorist Niels Bohr; Werner Heisenberg, who with a certitude established the certainty of his principle of uncertainty; Galileo, one of the few of his time who did not consider himself the center of the universe; and Richard Feynman, who advanced quantum electrodynamics and said things like, "A scientist looking at nonscientific problems is just as dumb as the next guy." Rounding out the final three are Paul Dirac, who discovered anti-matter, without which the Enterprise would have had the velocity of a river barge; Erwin Schrodinger, who discovered particles do the wave; and Ernest Rutherford, who concluded the nucleus of the atom is positively positive.

And I recall that, when Einstein died in 1955, the autopsy doctor put his brain in a jar for purposes of seeing what made him so smart. 23 years later, a reporter was assigned to find Einstein's brain and tracked it to two mason jars in a cardboard box labeled "cider" in a corner of the autopsy doctor's office in Wichita, following which the doctor reluctantly turned them over to others for scientific studies, the most recent of which was concluded in 1999. Sandra Witelson of McMaster University in Ontario found anomalies in Einstein's parietal lobes. They were larger than in other brains examined, and a groove which separates two portions of this area was absent, possibly allowing his neurons to make more connections and allowing him to visualize theory and translate it into abstract mathematics, supporting his own story that he developed his theory of relativity by daydreaming what it would be like to ride through the universe on a beam of light.

Which leads us to Johns Hopkins med school where Dr. Godfrey Pearlson has concluded the reason men are better in spatial conceptualization and physics than women (and the reason Einstein was better than most anybody), is because men have a bigger Inferior Parietal Lobe, IPL, than women, and that other men could only wish their IPLs were as big as Einstein, the Dirk Digler of IPLs. Anyhow, the John's Hopkins findings were that the Inferior Parietal Lobes on men are bigger on the left side of the brain while women's are bigger on the right, explaining women's superiority in areas such as language skills and remembering birthdays of third cousins.

Medical science---inching ever-closer to determining how in the world women can walk right by the pegboard-and-hook section at Home Depot without so much as slowing down for a look-see, whereas it would not occur to men to make flowers out of the radishes.

We Should Live So Long

When I read the Reuters news story datelined Vancouver, about a man who went to a lecture on life-after-death and he accidentally bumped the chair of a man next to him as he became seated, and the other man took out a knife and stabbed him and returned to listening to the lecture, at which the man who was stabbed staggered outside and went to a hospital to have his stab wound attended to, it recalled to mind another Reuters story of recent days in which a prisoner in Dublin's Mountjoy Prison stabbed his cellmate to death in his sleep because of his insufferable snoring. And together they serve to remind us that there are alternative ways of looking at most anything, because it can be said that the bad news is the first stabbing victim, who survived, still knows nothing of whether there is, in fact, life after death, while the good news is that the second stabbing victim, who did not survive, does.

And cogitating upon life and death moved me to phone up scientist Robert Lanza of Advanced Cell Technology in Worcester, Massachusetts, whose work has produced a half-dozen cloned cows, the cells of which are much younger than their chronological age, which means that their cells divide and reproduce just like baby cells instead of aging cells and hold out the potential for these cows to becoming the oldest living cows in cowdom. And he told me the potential exists for replicating the technique in humans; to the degree one's lifetime may be doubled, in that he sees 200 as the outside age for humans unless they can discover how to rejuvenate the brain as they can the other organs.

And doubling one's span of years means a whole rethinking of what should be done with that span of years, in that it certainly makes less sense to buy the term life insurance when one has two centuries to build equity in whole life. The technology is nearly there, I am told, to clone the cells in, say, aging knee cartilage, turn back the cellular clock in the laboratory, and inject one's own rejection-free youthful cells back into the knee, restoring to a septuagenarian the knee flexibility of a 20 year-old. This would be therapeutic cloning, not whole-human cloning, and thus available soon without ethical conflict to those who can afford it, which fits neatly into my plans for the next 200 million dollar Big Game jackpot.

In that slightly more than one-third of the sands of time remain in my hourglass, I would normally be inclined to take the lump-sum pay-out of somewhere in the neighborhood of 100+ million dollars (and a fine neighborhood it is, too, with long, tree-shaded driveways and four-car garages and lovely landscaping and balconies with a view of palm trees and the outer islands). Peel off another 28% to cover federal tax and 3% state tax, and one is left with the not-inconsiderable pile of 70 million dollars which one could park in a money-market account at four per-cent interest and still withdraw from the ATM 2.8 million a year without scuffing the principal. However, could I live for an additional century, it would make far greater sense to take the entire 200 million-dollar annuity pay-out of seven million, six hundred ninety-two thousand, three hundred seven dollars and sixty cents each year for 26 years. Because the difference is nearly five million dollars a year additional, and Dr. Lanza of Advanced Cell Technology assures me the cost of the cell-cloning required to restore youthful vigor to my organs, immune system, tissue, and flesh would likely be far less than one million per annum.

What could be better than being rich enough to become young enough to enjoy being rich and young? It was Euripides who wrote, "Youth is the best time to be rich." I teeter, sadly, at the threshold of an age, of which it is said that, when faced with a variety of temptations, one chooses the one that gets one home the earliest. From Ponce de León through James Thurber (who lobbied, when he was 65, for a fifteen-month year, in that it would adjust his age to 48), man has yearned for a youth restorative, which Advanced Cell Technology claims to have achieved. Just think what living for 200 years will mean to mankind, aside from doubling the word count in our obituaries. And one need not win the lottery to be rich in a span of 200 years, in that just two thousand dollars, invested in a triple-A instrument returning 7% interest would, in 99 years, yield one point six million dollars. And if one may be youthful for a hundred years, having the extra time to become proficient in French makes all the difference in deciding whether to relocate to Martinique.

The Secret Lives of Lima Beans

I have always liked lima beans, and it is neither helpful nor contributory to my enjoyment of them to discover they possess feelings. One should not have to consider the emotional states of vegetables, wouldn't you agree? It is in the Journal Nature that I read how lima bean plants send out distress signals when they find themselves in jeopardy.

To be frank, I have allowed my subscription to Nature to lapse, in that the annual rate has climbed to 159 dollars, an outlay I cannot justify for the perusal of articles with titles such as, "An intrinsic but cell-non-autonomous defect in GATA-1-overexpressing mouse erythroid cells," or "Quasi-planar nucleus structure in apoferritin crystallization." Had this magazine a crossword puzzle, it would doubtless be a really hard one. So I visit Nature's web site, where they permit, at no charge, the reading of an article's first paragraph, which is how I came to the story with the title, "Herbivory-induced volatiles elicit defense genes in lima bean leaves," which recounts the study by Junji Takabayashi and colleagues at Kyoto University, which discovered that lima beans issue a general alert when visited by spider mites.

I might point out that, like the potato, the history of the lima bean is the history of civilization. The fabled Incas of the Andes built their empire across Peru, Bolivia, Ecuador, and portions of Colombia, Chile and

Argentina over a period of 800 years, as a result of a stable food supply with potatoes and legumes as its foundation. The lima bean is more correctly pronounced Lima (lee-ma) after the capitol of Peru, founded by the ruthless conquistador Francisco Pizarro, whom the Incas perceived as not a nice man when he captured their emperor, collected a roomful of gold as ransom for his release, then killed the chief anyway and enslaved everybody else. Beans were unknown in the pre-Columbian old world and were a taste sensation as well as prized for their preservability and portability, and with dried beans large armies could be deployed to wage wars and conduct conquests. Lima beans are possessed of iron, phosphorus, zinc, protein, folate, magnesium and potassium; chock-full of fiber, low in calories and cholesterol-free, and might be called "nature's perfect superfood," were they not also possessed of the crowded-elevator-embarrassment property attributed to the family of musical fruits. The world's oldest lima beans have been discovered in a Peruvian cave in highlands north of Lima, dating to 8,000 BC in the Pleistocene. More than 53 thousand acres of U.S. soil at this very moment are home to lima beans, much of that in the Red River Valley of North Dakota, King of Lima Beans, whereas the Lima Bean Queen is crowned annually at the Lima Bean Festival in West Cape May, New Jersey.

Anyway, according to the journal Nature, when scientists in Kyoto are not marshalling their resources in an effort to deal with Gamera, they are loosing a plague of spider mites onto lima bean plants to see what happens, and what happens is, when the spider mite begins eating the lima leaves, the plant emits chemicals into the air which alert their neighbors to the danger, and their neighbors switch on a gene which produces a chemical which makes the plants less tasty to spider mites. In addition, the lima bean plant which is being nibbled upon by the spider mite (Tetranychus urticae), manufactures a chemical scent, which perfumes the air in its vicinity, specifically attracting another bigger kind of benign mighty mite with an appetite for spider mites.

There is likely much more interesting intelligence about the secret lives of lima beans which I was prohibited from learning by virtue of the ten dollars the Nature web site demands to view the entire article. But it is evident that lima beans are in constant communication with one another for purposes of nine-one-one'ing other lima beans about imminent danger.

Sadly, lima beans are in no imminent danger at my house, in that my wife and son share the conviction the Phaseolus limensis is not an actual food. And it is somewhat off-putting to learn lima beans are, to a degree, sentient beings, as it makes one less desirous of plundering their pods and eating their eggs.

Animal Kingdom Kings of Comedy

I once had an interesting conversation with the monkey woman Jane Goodall, who is not a monkey woman in the sense of, "She's inside, The Monkey Woman, alive, livin' and breathin'---How does she live, that po' little thing?" And who is also not the one who was killed by poachers in Africa. You are thinking of Sigourney Weaver.

Ms. Goodall is an animal behaviorist who has lived with the chimpanzees of the Gombe Stream National Park in Tanzania for forty years and has written extensively about Flo and Fifi and Freud and Frodo and Flint and Flick and the rest of her fricative-rich forest family, and was conducting a first-of-its-kind symposium among the top specialists in the behaviors of the major species of large-brained animals such as whales and gorillas and dolphins and elephants and lions and parrots. Never before had experts gathered together to compare whale songs with bird songs, and chimp hunting styles with lion hunting styles and killer whale culture with macaque culture in order to compare the social and emotional makeup of animals possessed with brains large enough to engage in behaviors inherently cerebral but not quite developed to the degree they exercise any discretion whatsoever about defecating outdoors in public.

I acquired press credentials and attended seminars with titles such as, "Social Cognition and Cooperation in the Spotted Hyena," and "Society and Culture of the Sperm Whale," and "Dolphins Learn Individualistic Whistles to Maintain Individual-Specific Social Relationships," in which it was learned that scientists have found that dolphins teach and learn, and pick up intricate vocal signals from one another believed to be the precursor of language, and that this demonstrates they are even smarter than previously believed, although not to the point they could beat us at Parcheesi. And scientists argued about the comparative IQs of chimps and dolphins which Jane Goodall called comparing apples and oranges because you put a chimp in the deep ocean and the dolphin is going to look smarter, but she is obviously biased toward chimps, because she says chimpanzees share 98.6% of their DNA with humans, with the remaining 1.4% the DNA which sets humans apart as the only species capable of constructing a good Long Island Iced Tea.

And there was a lecture delivered by a Dutch researcher by the name of Dr. Jan van Hooff, entitled, "The Jovial Chimp;" comparing what he calls the "primate play-face," with the human laugh, which moved me to inquire of Ms. Goodall whether she had seen behaviors suggesting that apes have a sense of humor? And she told me about Koko, the signing western lowland gorilla, who was, one day, met with a new greenhorn research student who revealed a white cloth and signed, asking Koko the color, to which Koko signed "red," at which the student told Koko she knew better than that, and what was the color, to which Koko signed "red" again, to which the student, believing Koko was being obstreperous, signed that Koko would therefore not be rewarded with her banana and fruit juice, to which Koko grabbed the white cloth, picked off a minute red fiber which had attached itself in the dryer, and signed over and over, "Red, red, red," as she bared her teeth and hooted loudly," which, I might suggest, falls somewhere on the evolution of comedy timeline, between Uncle Bob pretending his thumb is your nose, and the punch line, "Because he wanted to see time fly." And Ms. Goodall described joking behavior she had witnessed at Gombe, suggesting that what is funny to a chimpanzee is what we would call teasing, and the more peeved and annoyed a chimp's victim becomes, the more hilarious the chimpanzee finds the exercise. So there is joking among the higher primates, skewed intellectually less toward a Mort Sahl or David Steinberg and more toward Adam Sandler.

And I asked Jane Goodall if she'd heard the one about the marine biologist who genetically engineered dolphins to live forever if only they were fed a diet of seagulls, and finding the cupboard bare of seagulls, the biologist went out to trap more, and returning with his catch, he came upon a pride of lions asleep in the road and keeping ever so quiet, so as not to awaken them, he stepped gingerly over them, to find himself arrested for transporting gulls across sedate lions for immortal porpoises; and she said she hadn't, and I offered to write it down for her but she said that wouldn't be necessary, so I assumed she committed it to memory.

Chapter 3—Stooges and Other Icons

Waiting for Mike Anthony

When I was a boy, lying on my back in the green grass looking up into the blue Ohio sky, my aspirations were absent of materialism and simple; generally associated with horses and branding irons and chuckwagons and red and white neckerchiefs useful for turning around when one had a notion to rob the stage.

But I would undergo a Mr. Hyde transformation into a money-mad avaricious greedy-Gus every Wednesday night when my favorite show came on at 9 eastern on CBS just before I've Got a Secret. It was the one where, every week in the opening scene, eccentric gazillionaire John Beresford Tipton would be seated in the study of his fabulously enormous estate, Silverstone, now and again fingering the chess pieces before him, before summoning his personal secretary, Mike Anthony. And John Beresford Tipton would impart some bromide such as, "You know, Mike, H.L. Mencken said that "The chief value of money lies in the fact that one lives in a world in which it is overestimated," to which we impatient young viewers would respond, "Yeah, yeah, just give him the envelope," inside of which we knew to be nestled a crisp cashier's check in the amount of one million dollars, taxes paid. At which point Mike Anthony would convey the envelope to the recipient who would invariably wreck his life with it or otherwise prove that money isn't everything and can't buy happiness and "I don't care too much for money, cause money can't buy me love," blah, blah, blah, blah.

Which I thought of when I received a copy of Modern Maturity Magazine, published by the American Association of Retired Persons, whose acronym, AARP, is pronounced as letters and not as the sound of a cartoon upchuck. And I wish to make it clear as a window on the OCD ward that I receive Modern Maturity because I am a journalist, not because I, in any way, am prepared to subscribe to a lifestyle remotely associated with maturity. And this periodical surveyed its readership, 80% of which say having a lot of money makes people greedy and uppity. 75% think rich people are insensitive to others, and fully one third answer "no" when the question is "Would you like to be wealthy?" Defining terms, the survey shows more than half of mature Americans, less youthful than myself, would consider themselves wealthy with less than five hundred thousand dollars in total assets, while a mere 8% say it takes a million dollars to be rich.

And I am gladful for this elder generation of Americans, unspoiled by avarice, and, on the flight we all share bound for life's inevitable and certain mortal destination, content to sit in Row 34C. Because others of us aspire to the comfort of an exit aisle or a bulkhead at the very least, and to recline beyond the forward curtains given the opportunity. A million dollars seems the very minimum one must maintain in one's account to be considered wealthy, as it was Lady Nancy Astor who said, "A man who has a million dollars is as well off as if he were rich." It is the mature generation, which we, whose modern maturity continues to ripen, will replace as AARP subscribers, who wrongly subscribe to a suspicion of wealth and are reluctant to participate in its acquisition.

We, their children, have no such allergy, and came away from The Millionaire with a different message from its usual cautionary tale, convinced the only mistake was in giving the money to the wrong person, by which, I meant at the time, someone who was not me. Who Wants to be a Millionaire? The man in the mirror, that's who. Because we see wisdom in the remark by J. Paul Getty that, "The meek shall inherit the earth, but not its mineral rights," and in the philosophy of Albert Camus, who declared, "It is spiritual snobbery that makes people think they can be happy without money." Money is greatly to be desired, for, as Bret Maverick's old grandpappy used to say, "Marry for money, my little sonny, a rich man's joke is always funny."

By the way, the voice of millionaire John Beresford Tipton, whose face was never seen, was Chicago born Paul Frees, whose voice is also the ghost host in the Disney parks' Haunted Mansions, and is most of the pirate voices in Pirates of the Caribbean, and was TV's Ludwig Von Drake and the narrator in the Shaggy Dog and the radio announcer in The Absent Minded Professor, and who was also the voice of Boris Badenov and also Nell's father Inspector Fenwick on Dudley Do-Right, and the voices of John and George in the Beatles cartoons and the original Pillsbury Doughboy. And those voices turned Paul Frees into a millionaire, one of the nouveau riche. And there are those who turn up their noses at the nouveau riche, but I subscribe to the sentiments of whoever said, "Better to be nouveau than never to have been riche at all."

Niagara Falls

You may have seen where a Texas lawyer claimed that his client shot his girlfriend three times when he thought she was going to say the words "New Jersey," because the words "New Jersey" always trigger, in this man, a rage reaction which renders him berserk. Witnesses during the trial used flash cards so as not to speak the words "New Jersey" aloud in the presence of the defendant. And this recalled to my mind the greatest contribution to American culture rendered by my favorite underwear logo dancing fruit, and here is why:

A few months ago, I took Anita to see Niagara Falls, and as we drew near, she observed a road sign and read the words, "Niagara Falls," to which, without missing a beat, I recited, in a voice resonating with stentorian drama: "SLOWLY, I TURNED! STEP BY STEP, INCH BY INCH...," and cackled at my own cleverness, while, in the same moment, Anita imagined me a certified nitwit. So it fell to me to tell her the story of Joey Faye.

Joey Faye was a burlesque comic who was born in New York in 1909, the year Teddy Roosevelt shot a rhinoceros and Mary Pickford's salary as a film star was raised to 40 dollars a week. Joey Faye made his living as a slapstick second banana and was later promoted from banana to a bunch of grapes as an original TV commercial Fruit of the Loom Guy. But his seminal endowment to the art of western civilization was his authorship of the "Slowly I Turned" sketch.

And this is it in a nutshell: Two men pass on the street. In a neighborly way, one says "Hiya, pal," to which the other stops suddenly and allows as how he hasn't heard that word in years, since the day his life was ruined when he came home to a note revealing that his wife was stolen by another man. Consumed with revenge, he describes his pursuit of the duplicitous Jezebel and her perfidious paramour. And when the stranger inquires where the jealous man caught up with his rival, the answer is Niagara Falls. And it turns out that hearing the words "Niagara Falls" compels the ranting man to reenact his violent confrontation with his wife's lover, recounting that "Slowly, I turned, step by step" he approached his prey and, in a delusional frenzy, beats the pleasant stranger to the ground, ripping his clothes, before regaining control of himself. Helped to his feet by the apologetic head case, the pleasant stranger expresses his consternation that such violence could be triggered by the mere mention of Niagara Falls, which triggers another maniacal bruising, clothes-shredding episode. And as the unhinged husband departs, raving incoherently, and the stranger is laboring to restore his appearance, the fugitive boyfriend appears and replies to the pleasant stranger's off-handed greeting that he, too, hasn't heard the word "pal" in years. And the boyfriend's eyes glaze with deranged fury as he recalls how he was pursued by a jealous husband, and the stranger surmises aloud that the pursuit ended in Niagara Falls; which, of course, invites another psychotic shirt-tattering assault. Suddenly, the husband returns, and the two adversaries confront one another and the pleasant stranger is incredulous when the two men shake hands like buddies, and he asks them if they've forgotten what happened in Niagara Falls, which causes them both to wheel toward him and chant: NIAGARA FALLS! SLOWLY I TURNED, STEP BY STEP, INCH BY INCH…"

And every boy in my school knew it by heart, because this sketch was stolen and performed by Abbot and Costello and Danny Thomas and Lucy and Ricky. But every American male would agree that the definitive version belongs to The Three Stooges, who performed it, with incomparable virtuosity, in 1944's "Gents Without Cents." And we boys would reprise this routine often at recess, and though it was customary for male youth to aspire to the role of Curly; in the case of the Niagara Falls sketch the more prudent among us elected to be Moe and the part of the pleasant stranger usually fell to Stumo, whose smart pill prescription was always needful of a refill, to speak "Niagara Falls" and eat dirt.

And Joey Faye's masterpiece provided me solid evidence that, when I married Anita, I became the most fortunate of men. You see, when I told her the story and confided that I surely would like to see that routine again, she ordered up the Columbia TriStar DVD of

Three Stooges shorts that includes this classic bit. And she did this for me, with full awareness of the consequences; that she would unavoidably acquire a scar on her permanent record in the sorority of womanhood so shamefully monstrous as to cause any self-respecting sentient being with double-X chromosomes to weep. Because, when one buys something on Amazon.com---forever after, one will be informed upon one's return: "If you liked The Three Stooges' anthology, 'Healthy, Wealthy and Dumb,' you'll love 'Dumb and Dumber,' or 'Dude Where's My Car?', or 'Bill and Ted's Bogus Journey,' or 'Abbot and Costello Meet the Wolfman.' Or Larry, Curly and Moe in 'All the World's a Stooge.'" Greater love hath no woman.

Anyhow, the jury didn't buy the Texas lawyer's defense that the words "New Jersey" caused his client to shoot his girlfriend. And the papers called the gambit the word-rage strategy, but I suggest legal scholars call it the Joey Faye Defense. By the way, Joey Faye died in an Actor's Home in 1997. In New Jersey.

And Robert Blake as Little Beaver

When first I heard that Robert Blake had been charged with conspiring to kill his lonely-hearts, celebrity-bilking, con-artist wife---it recalled to my mind (as it likely did to yours) fond memories of the golden age of white actors playing Indians, in the same spirit in which Hollywood believed that if one pulled the skin beside Marlon Brando's eyes back real tight in *Teahouse of the August Moon*, he would pass for Okinawan.

The real McCoy bona fide red man was hired to fall off horses circling wagon trains, but, for the most part, the meaty roles went to painted Caucasians, with the exception of Jay Silverheels, whose roles between 1950 and 1960 were, in chronological order: Geronimo, Little Crow, Tecumseh, Lead warrior, Joe Arrow, Indian, Running Wolf, Geronimo, Chingachgook, Red Cloud, Satanta, Spotted Bear, Cajou, Yellow Hawk, Yacqui, Taos, Black Buffalo, Beeteia, Tonto, Geronimo, Indian Joe, Tonto, and Tonto.

Jeff Chandler was Cochise in *Broken Arrow*, following which, he was Cochise in *Battle at Apache Pass*, after which, he was Cochise in *Taza, Son of Cochise*, despite having been born in Brooklyn. And on the *Broken Arrow* TV series Cochise was Michael Ansara, who was born in Syria, married Barbara Eden, and played Iron Jacket in *Texas Across the River*, in which Joey Bishop played Dean Martin's Indian sidekick, Kronk. And in 1962's *Geronimo*, Geronimo was Chuck Connors. And in *Apache*, following the surrender of Geronimo, the last Apache warrior is Massai, who is Burt Lancaster. And Chief Crazy Horse, in *Died They with Their Boots On*, is Anthony Quinn. And in *Cactus Jack*, Nervous Elk was Paul Lynde. And in *Cockeyed Cowboys of Calico County*, Mickey Rooney played Indian Tom and Crazy Foot was Iron Eyes Cody. And some might dispute the inclusion of Iron Eyes Cody in a list of non-Indians playing Indians, since he was famous as the teary-eyed official Native-American anti-littering poster boy. Submitted for your consideration: A 1996 expose by a New Orleans newspaper that proclaimed Iron Eyes Cody's birth certificate, bearing the name Oscar DeCorti, reveals he came into this world a full-blooded Italian.

Anyway, in my favorite western, *The Searchers*, the Comanche renegade, Scar, was played by Henry Brandon, who was christened, at his birth in Berlin, Germany, as Heinrich Von Kleinbach. And the Comanche, Notah, in 1969's *Comanche Blanco* was William Shatner. And in John Wayne's *The War Wagon*, Levi Walking Bear was Howard Keel, who was Frank Butler in *Annie Get Your Gun*, and in the *Annie Get Your Gun* revival touring company, Sitting Bull was Larry Storch, whom, it will be recalled, served time at Fort Courage, near the encampment of a tribe whose chief, Wild Eagle, was Frank DeKova, who was Chief Chattez in the movie *Arrowhead* (where his Apache son was Jack Palance), and was Chief Red Hawk in *The Lone Ranger*, and Yellow Elk in *White Squaw*, and Red Cloud in *Run of the Arrow*, and White Eagle in *Johnny Firecloud*.

And way before he was *Baretta* or the Mexican urchin who sold Humphrey Bogart a lottery ticket in *The Treasure of the Sierra Madres*, Robert Blake made twenty-three movies cast in the role of Little Beaver---the Indian boy sidekick of *Red Ryder*---despite his having been baptized in Nutley, New Jersey, as Michael James Vavencio Gubitosi. And *Red Ryder* was Wild Bill Elliott in the first sixteen *Red Ryders* and Allan Lane was *Red Ryder* in the last seven, but Robert Blake was Little Beaver in all of them. And Robert Blake went on to revisit his Native-American roots in 1969's *Tell Them Willie Boy Is Here*, in which he is Willy Boy, the fugitive Indian tracked by Robert Redford, whereas Red

Ryder went on to become the Daisy 111, model 40 Carbine with which America's youth aspired to shoot its eye out. Extra credit: What was Little Beaver's pony's name? If you said, "Papoose," you may now delete it from your hippocampus, as it will never come up again.

Not a Small World After All

In 1964 my dad packed us into the station wagon and we headed that wagon eastward ho from the state which is "round on the ends and hi in the middle," Ohio, to Flushing Meadows and the New York World's Fair. But all I can remember of the long ride home, the length of the Pennsylvania Turnpike, was my sister in the back seat singing over and over the diabolically infective lyrics of the song implanted into our cerebral cortexes in the Pepsi Cola Pavilion, which was the first appearance anywhere of the Disney designed, "It's a Small World," ride, which was subtitled at the World's Fair, "A Salute to UNICEF." The one whose final lyric was "There is just one moon and one golden sun. And a smile means friendship to everyone. Although mountains are high. And the oceans divide. It's a small world after all."

Which was an effort to ingrain, in America's children, a tolerance for diversity to address the warning in the Rogers and Hammerstein's lyric that, "You've got to be taught, before it's too late. Before you are six, or seven, or eight. To hate all the people your relatives hate. You've got to be carefully taught." A theme explored later by Sylvester Stewart in his 1968 lyrics observing that, "There is a blue one who can't accept the green one. For living with a fat one, who's trying to be a skinny one. And different strokes, for different folks. And so on and so on and scooby dooby dooby." Which was a theme reworked by DePeche Mode in the musical question, "People are people. So why should it be, You and I should get along so awfully?" And the theme running through these compositions is one of shared universal commonality, a globalism indoctrination which takes years to unlearn, to discover we are not all the same and only partly because of Haggis. Scotland celebrates the anniversary of poet Robert Burns' birthday by consuming the minced heart, lungs, and liver of a sheep mixed with solid kidney fat and boiled in the animal's stomach, an item to X-out on the list of things we share with the Scots. Elsewhere, in the Russian city of Pskov, four men killed a friend in a drunken brawl, then cut up his flesh and boiled it and delivered it to a canner who put it up in tins labeled fresh meat. Meanwhile, in the Spanish town of Manganeses de la Polvarosa, for the first time in history, the annual goat hurling was cancelled after officials warned anyone throwing a goat off the top of the church steeple would be fined. For a century, drunken revelers at this fiesta would throw a goat off the tower into a canvas sheet held fireman-style by others below. To those who would sing, "There's so much that we share, that it's time we're aware, it's a small world," et cetera, I might point out that, in the Wakayama province of Japan, each village has a shrine called a hari kuyo where interment services are held for broken sewing needles, in the belief that, since the broken sewing needles died in service to their masters, and had worked hard all their lives, it is just that they be laid to rest on a soft bed of tofu. Clearly, the peoples of the world are possessed of cultural ticks unshared. For example The Kenya Times reports local prostitutes raced to Lake Victoria upon hearing that wildlife officials had killed a huge crocodile while hunting for a killer hippo. The prostitutes pushed and shoved trying to get to the carcass to cut off the crocodile's genitals, which are highly regarded as a strong love potion. Quoting the newspaper article, "The whores left disappointed after the wardens tied a boulder to the carcass and sank it to the bottom of the lake," unquote. Also, certain Indian yogis in the cult of Shiva, worship their own penises and engage in a religious observance called narachastra prayoga, which is Sanskrit for The Hand of Shiva. Which taken together is reason enough for gladness that the mountains are high and the oceans are wide, after all.

And I remember the Travelers Insurance pavilion had dioramas tracing the totality of history from the dinosaurs up to the Mercury and Gemini astronauts. And I recall enjoying the Dupont Chemical pavilion with its "Wonderful World of Chemistry" musical revue tracing in song and dance the history of chemistry from ancient Greece to what it declared was the greatest scientific breakthrough of the period: Polyester.

What Religion Were the Flintstones?

E-mailer Faye Lawrey writes about a matter that has perplexed her; a matter I will relate to you now. Ms. Lawrey had been reading about a woman in Georgia, who used to be visited annually by the Virgin Mary. This woman claimed that, each October 13, the Holy

Mother would appear at her farm, like in the movie *The Song of Bernadette*, which is the one with Lee J. Cobb and Vincent Price, with Linda Darnell playing the Virgin Mary without a screen credit. And thousands would pilgrimage to this farm each October 13, to hear the Georgia woman listen to the Holy message and then to repeat it to the public. And to Ms. Lawrey's question regarding her skepticism about the woman's ability to understand the Virgin's message, my answer was that yes, I do assume the Mother of God likely spoke Aramaic, as would have been the custom of the working trade from Nazareth, and that no, the farmer's wife in Georgia is not fluent in that ancient dialect, which was the parent of modern-day Arabic.

Having said that, I do believe we can assume that Holy Mary Mother of God can make herself understood in any language, as when we are watching Star Trek, and find ourselves understanding both Romulan and Cardassian.

And, as this matter set me to contemplate matters theological, I began to cogitate upon a question raised in my own mind a few days ago. I was watching *The Flintstones* over the weekend on the Cartoon Network. It was the special where Pebbles and Bamm-Bamm get married, and the minister who married them was wearing the collar of a cleric. Which gave me pause, since, after all, the Flintstones, as we all well know, are a modern Stone-Age family. And the Stone Age (or Paleolithic Period) dates from the appearance of early stone tools and record players using the beaks of birds as styluses -- or is it styli? And certainly the clerical collar is unmistakable as a trapping of the Christian religion, with its root word being, of course, Christ. As in, "Before Christ," which certainly even modern Stone-Age families indisputably were.

And we can trace the earliest origins of the Christian religion to the biblical patriarch, Abraham, father of the three great religions of Islam, Judaism and Christianity, who lived in the ancient city of Ur in Mesopotamia some 1300 or so years B.C. And even the oldest religion on earth, Hinduism, can be traced back no more than two thousand years before Christ, but I don't imagine any of us would view the Flintstones as remotely Hindu. No, there is no easy answer, and we must ultimately leave the answer to the question, "What religion were the Flintstones?" to the theologians.

In a related matter, E-mailer Donald Berger asked if I would settle an argument among friends at a bar, and declare, once and for all, who was hotter, Wilma or Betty? And I replied that, to me, among the Hanna Barbera stable of starlets, I have always had a soft spot for Jane Jetson; capable yet vulnerable. And speaking of that, I can't help but wonder whatever happened to Astro, and whether he ever got help for his speech impediment. You know, when he would say, "Ruh, roh Rorge." And you know, if he could pronounce the G at the end of George, I would think he could be taught to pronounce the G at the beginning of the word too.

It is not common knowledge that the original Astro died in a plane crash on his way to a benefit, along with his constant companion at the time, Paddlefoot, pet of the late Clutch Cargo. They had been linked romantically, but it was the early 60s, and they were both boys and cartoon character canines had yet to come out of the kennel. His role was later taken over by a young Scooby Doo, but it was like Shemp in the Three Stooges. It wasn't the same.

Our Friend the Atom

The plan to store America's radioactive waste in Nevada actually includes a message to archeologists of the future. If accomplished, the Yucca Mountain tunnels could hold seventy thousand tons of radioactive material, such as plutonium, which will remain toxic for a hundred thousand years. And for those of us who have trouble recalling our pin numbers, it is reasonable that one day nobody will remember it's there. So the government will pay for construction at Yucca Mountain of twenty-ton granite spikes engraved with warnings in seven languages and will bury thousands of other warning tablets all around notifying diggers in the distant future of the presence of the lethal nuclear byproducts.

And it's apropos the site should be in Nevada, not far from the area where scientific men and women refined the technology to turn Our Friend the Atom into the safe and inexpensive source of plentiful energy we have come to know as the American Nuclear Power Industry. It was Albert Einstein who said that nuclear chain reactions need not bring about the destruction of man any more than the discovery of matches, and also that he didn't know with what weapons man would fight World War III, but World War IV would be fought with sticks and stones; evidence that Albert Einstein was, right up until his death in 1955, America's most prolific creator of quotations. Of his General Theory of Relativity he said "when you are courting a girl an hour seems like a second, and when you sit on a cinder a second seems like an hour," which was, years later, refined by Steven Wright, who told the police officer, "Yes, I was going 75 miles an hour, but I was on the road much less than an hour," which subsequently raised the question, "If you are traveling faster than the speed of light, what happens when you turn on your headlights?" But of course Einstein's most profound bequest to the modern age was his proof that the mass of a body is a measure of its energy content; whose formula led directly to the invention of the atom bomb.

Sixty-five miles northwest of the Dancing Fountains at the Bellagio, lies the largest secured area in the United States; a thirteen hundred square-mile proving ground called the Nevada Test Site. Larger than the state of Rhode Island, this is where the Atomic Energy Commission detonated dozens of nuclear weapons, and where, until the Limited Test Ban Treaty of 1963 drove testing underground, often the only clouds in the arid sky were in the shape of mushrooms. This was during the era in which the 16mm documentaries, screened by the audio-visual club in social studies, would show the blood-red stain of international Communism spreading across Europe and Asia. This was the 1950s, before the biggest brains in nuclear physics discovered what every schoolchild knows today: that nuclear testing makes things grow real big.

It was at the Nevada Test Site that Lt. Colonel Glenn Manning leaped from a trench to help the pilot of a plane that crashed, and was caught in the Plutonium blast that shredded his clothes and turned him into what the papers called the Amazing Colossal Man, a condition which left him seated uncomfortably on his teeny bed trying to read a book the size of a Chiclet and feeling frustrated for having a sex organ that could fit in a cattle car and a fiancé the size of a radish. As he grew to fifty feet, his heart and circulatory system failed to keep up and he gradually lost his mind as a result of the reduced blood supply to his brain, and, insane, he went on a rampage through Las Vegas, committing architectural battery until the army doctors jabbed him with a giant syringe, which he picked up and flung through the chest of a soldier like a dartsman in a Welsh pub. And, ultimately, he fell off the Hoover Dam into the churning water below, and was never seen again. Until the sequel, "War of the Colossal Beast," where they made his face hideously burned and scarred hoping we won't notice it wasn't the same actor.

This sort of nuclear accident happened all too often during the era of above ground testing, which also awakened the slumbering Rhedosaurus from the arctic *in Beast from 20,000 Fathoms* and the giant ants in *Them!* and Godzilla and Rodan and the giant Octopus in *Monster from the Ocean Floor*. It was only rarely when nuclear testing went awry that the reverse would result, as in *the Incredible Shrinking Man*, primarily because scientists discovered it was much less expensive to make the props really small than the reverse. Of course, the superpowers have since foresworn the madness of nuclear proliferation, and since the nuclear weapons testing moratorium of 1992, the Department of Energy Nevada Test Site has been used for other classified military projects not involving extraterrestrial aircraft; swear on a stack of Bibles.

The Drum Major

Driving past a band practice on a high school football field near my house, I was reminded of a correspondence I conducted with a young man some years ago, which began with the following E-mail, quoting: "My name is Ryan Bergauer, and I live in Texas. My uncle loves your Dave's Raves and pointed me to the web site. Now I love 'em, too. I have a favor to ask. I know that you are probably very busy, but I am running for Drum Major of my band, and need to come up with a really catchy speech. Do you have suggestions or neat anecdotes I could use?"

And I replied thusly: Ryan, I am never too busy to encourage young people to become drum majors, because the tradition of men throwing sticks is deeply embedded in humankind's genetic double helix. It was in the misty dawn of proto-human prehistory that the first antediluvian hominid came down from the trees and picked up a stick and walked out of the forest onto the plains taking that first step and waving that stick and leading the march of subsequent human history. It was, of course, a silent march, because it would be many eons before the invention of the horn section blowing "Lay Lady Lay" to the staccato tattoo of the snares.

And marching to percussion is a Texan's birthright, as witness the incident on the streets of Laredo where that cowboy was wrapped in white linen and cold as the clay who delivered the clammy exhortation to "beat the drum slowly and play the fife lowly, and play the Dead March as you carry me along," although an up-tempo rythym would better lend itself to the brief moments at halftime before the opposing band attempts "A Salute to Iron Butterfly."

But in your campaign, I would counsel you to soft peddle one's natural bias against actual band members and other lower life forms. Though it may be true, it would be a violation of *noblesse oblige* to riddle, "What's the difference between sophomore French horn players and gas powered wood chippers? Gas powered wood chippers sound better in small ensembles." A Drum Major is an aristocrat; a high-booted blueblood Galahad of the gridiron, and from the troglodyte Cro-Magnon man of age-encrusted time primeval through iron-age peat-burning man to Abercrombie & Fitch-man, a homo sapiens' prestige is related directly to the number of sticks in his hands. One stick. You are the leader of the allied expeditionary forces pointing to a map outlining the Normandy invasion. One stick. You are the director of the Berlin Symphony Orchestra, conducting Wagner's Ring of the Nibelung. One stick. You are the Drum Major. Two sticks, you sit in the back and beat on animal skins. Three sticks. You are the juggler at the Renaissance Faire. A bag full of sticks. You are Jordan Spieth choking at the Masters.

And there is nothing so resplendent as a drum major. The Drum Major is the necessity which required the invention of the word: resplendent. From the tip of his tasseled boots, up the length of his snug riding breeches with the gold stripes up the sides, past the waist-sash clearly visible beneath the short military jacket with tails and trefoil sleeve-trim and shaggy golden epaulets, to the soaring top of his busby held snugly by a chin strap with accessory cords draped beneath the feathery plume, he is every inch the inspiring image of leadership. But let me counsel you away from the sequined diagonal sash. In your position attracting a cheerleader is a tough sell as it is.

And I can certainly understand a young man experiencing a quickening of the pulse as one lifts, from its velvet blanket in its leather case, the Peacock Mace with its jet black shaft and chromium ball and tip, and its streaming military cords of maroon and gold. Such an artifact would make any healthy human hanker to throw one's head back and lift one's knee chest high and strut. This is a Drum Major. Because we all aspire, at some time in our lives, to be the leader of the band, and to know that at one's back are 76 trombones with 110 cornets close at hand.

Who are followed by rows and rows of the finest virtuosos,
The cream of every famous band.
With the copper bottom timpani in horse platoons,
Thundering, thundering all along the way.
Double bell euphoniums and big bassoons,
Each bassoon, having its big, fat say.

And I concluded my remarks of more than 24 years ago with these words: And Ryan, I don't know that you will achieve your aspiration, but I do know this: that whoever is leading the band, and whatever band it is, it will be marching to the Theme from *Titanic*.

Central Casting

Often the Internet is like when Alice was making her way through the chessboard land beyond the looking glass and encountered the White Queen who lived her life backwards so that her memory could work both ways, and when the suggestion was made that some of her notions were impossible, the Queen declared she had more than once believed in as many as six impossible things before breakfast.

On the Internet one is likely to encounter a half-dozen surreal improbabilities before breakfast and for me, today, a prime example was Plaster of Paradise. I was doing a search on Alfred Hitchcock's *Rear Window*, and up popped Castroom.com, home to Plaster of Paradise; a site inhabited by people who can't stop obsessing about wearing plaster casts for no reason.

And I was surprised to learn that there exist among us, individuals who so envy those whose injured arms and legs are encased in plaster that they enthusiastically undertake to immobilize their own limbs. My search engine paused at Plaster of Paradise because it features pinup photographs of Jimmy Stewart in *Rear Window*; hip-to-toe cast, the caster's cast of choice.

Casters are those fetishists to whom getting plastered means something else entirely. The introduction, written by Bob, our host, explains, quoting, "Although for many of us there is a sexual element to casting, it is not primarily a sexual desire. Sure, sex can be wonderful in casts," enthuses Bob, who continues, "but so is toddling through the mall on crutches," unquote. Bob recounts his desire to wear casts from the age of 14, often daydreaming about how to effectuate an injury necessitating plaster encasement.

His site offers mail-order hospital-quality cast supplies and instructions for their application. He suggests those without ready access to casting paraphernalia insert their limbs into large PVC pipes as a temporary feel-good. Highly recommended is a product called Castblast, which shoots an aerosol spritz of talc through a long thin tube, inserted behind the cast to relieve itching for hours. Plaster of Paradise offers a primer on caster jargon, such as; "swinging a full-leg cast on crutches is 'riding the rock.'"

Featured in the photo gallery are stills from the MGM movie, *Paperback Romance*, in which both romantic leads wind up in leg casts straight out of central casting. Also pictured; photos from the episode of *Full House* when John Stamos fell off his motorcycle and wore casts on both arms. Also pictured; Susan Hayward in *With a Song in my Heart*, wearing a leg cast and entertaining an entire GI hospital ward audience in body casts. Pictured, too, are various *Simpson's* characters wearing casts, including Bart and Homer. From *Saved By the Bell*, a photograph of cast-wearing cast-member Slater.

I briefly entered the caster chat-room in which there were eleven participants expressing admiration for one in their midst who had just immobilized both his legs hip to ankle, but when a new arrival identified himself by the handle Casty, and said he was from Sweden, the creepiness factor caused me to click the heck out of there, and I flashed on the Three Dog Night admonition, "That ain't the way to have fun, son."

By the way, the reason I was doing a search on Alfred Hitchcock's *Rear Window*: I have confirmed the identity of the actor who portrays the nameless songwriter; forever noodling on his piano with a melody which drifts up to the ears of Jimmy Stewart as he casts his binoculared eyes around his courtyard apartment neighbors' windows. This bit actor, an actual songwriter, had a hit in 1951 with "Come-On-a My-House," co-written with his lyric-writing uncle (who had refused the Pulitzer Prize for his play, "The Time of Your Life"), author William Saroyan; a Hit Parade collaboration which became a signature tune for Rosemary Clooney. But a duplication of this initial success eluded this tunesmith, who took a number of make-work jobs, including small parts in *Viva Zapata* and *Stalag 17*, until he fell upon the gimmick of speeding up his voice and harmonizing with himself, and he became Alvin, Simon, and Theodore, and the voice of David Seville whose *Chipmunk Song* went to number one and sold three and a half million copies in just five weeks in 1958, the same year he struck gold with the "Ting, tang, walla-walla bing-bang" number one song of that year, *Witch Doctor*. His name was Ross Bagdasarian, and I'm Kasey Kasem.

Cain and Abel and Zorro

It likely happened eons ago because I am sometimes oblivious to change, but it occurred to me as I read the comics this morning that Dennis the Menace is now going by his first name solo. The menace has gone out of the title, a vanishing phantom menace, leaving readers to recognize Dennis by his first name, as they already do Marmaduke and Blondie and Dilbert, joining the pantheon of public personalities achieving sufficient fame as to jettison their surnames and get by in the world as a forename like Jesus or Cher, although it can be argued that as a diminutive of Cherilyn, Cher was not actually her Christian name, although Jesus certainly was his.

And certainly there is nothing new about somebody going by a single name, especially when the world was new, back in the times when, after Abel was slain, Cain was on a very short list of suspects. And early men of letters were principally divided into men of nine letters, as were Aristotle and Sophocles and Euripides and Aeschylus and Confucius and men of five letters as were Aesop and Homer and Plato. And certain single names have been so admired and coveted by others that they have been acquired often enough that Roman numerals are required to differentiate between King Henrys and Pope Piuses although nobody would mistake Madonna for her namesake, or Mickey's Pluto for the Roman God of the underworld.

Heroic names, especially, often stand unsupported by a family name, in that it is unlikely that a priest ever spoke the words, "I baptize you Zorro, in the name of the Father, and the Son, and the Holy Ghost." Same with Tarzan and Batman. Literary second-bananas, too, would not have been nearly as effective with surnames, and by way of example I cite Chewbacca and Queequeg. And all Seven Dwarves.

Particularly suited to stand-alone names are those beginning with the letter G, as who will fail to immediately recognize the identities of Goliath, Garfield, Goofy, Gilligan and God? Or Godzilla? Some heroes of legend have more than one one-name. You can call him Ulysses or you can call him Odysseus, but don't call him late to Ithaca for the slaying of his wife's suitors. Somehow one senses that the golden age of one-named public figures has come and gone when one compares a Moses and an Abraham and a Socrates and a Diogenes and a Demosthenes and an Alexander to a Dino and a Fabian and a Fabio.

And in the 1960s, Dino hung out with Frank and Sammy, whereas in prehistoric times, Dino hung out with Fred and Barney. Not to be confused with the Barney who is today a purple sauropod. In the old west Trampas was Trampas and it didn't occur to anybody to ask, "Shane what?" No last names are recorded for Geronimo or Sacagawea.

There are hundreds of familiar first names we can announce have left the building without fear of confusion. Elvira and Kermit, Bert and Ernie, Dracula and Dumbo, Yoda and Booboo, Bluto and Oprah and Liberace and Yanni and Charo and Selena and Lulu and Coolio and Eminem and Enya and Sting and Bono and Bjork.

Some single names are long and foreign-sounding, such as Rasputin, and others are short and to the point, such as God.

Admittedly one's name can regrettably stereotype or typecast one, as it did Narcissus, in that it was Daffy Duck who once said, *"Because my name is Daffy, They think that I'm insane. Please pass the ketchup, I think it's going to rain! Oh, you can't bounce a meatball, Try with all your might. Turn on the radio, I want to fly a kite!"*

And many individuals elect to adopt new names because their given names might lead to confusion, which was the reason Francis Scott Key Fitzgerald preferred that you call him F. Scott, and why Albert Brooks became a Brooks because he felt Albert Einstein might be a distraction.

The Bay State Anthem and the Vulcan Adios

The Massachuset were the indigenous natives living in twenty Indian villages around Boston Bay, numbering some three thousand, in 1614, when Captain John Smith arrived with a shipment of viruses that dispatched three quarters of the resident population. When the Pilgrims arrived in 1620, they found fewer than 800 of the Massachuset still present, and set about inflicting respiratory infections to speed the attrition. When the Puritans settled in Boston in 1629, they counted fewer than 500 and set about distributing smallpox, which killed off most of the rest, but they persisted in small groups and the diluted blood of the Massachuset continues to pump in the veins of a small number of Bay Staters to this day. And I feel compelled to relate a peculiar association in my mind with the Commonwealth named for a nearly extinct tribe and it is that when I think of Massachusetts I think of the first science officer of the U.S.S. Enterprise and I'll tell you why.

Not long ago, I was endeavoring to ascertain, for an E-mailer, the origin, in Star Trek, of the spoken phrase,

"Live Long and Prosper," and found myself on hold at the Star Trek Fan Club based in Denver. And when you are on hold at the Star Trek Fan Club you hear various Star Trek themes interrupted periodically by a digital voice which says, "Please continue to stand by while we attempt to transport you to the first available docking bay." When I was, in time, docked with, I was told by an archivist, who looked it up, that the phrase first surfaced in episode one of the 1967 second season entitled, "Amok Time"; the one where Spock goes to Vulcan to get married but winds up having to fight Captain Kirk and where the phrase, "Live long and prosper, Spock," is spoken by the Vulcan high council member T'Pau to which Spock replies, "I shall do neither. I have killed my captain, and my friend."

Now, it turns out that this episode was written by the late science fiction writer Theodore Sturgeon, who was born Edward Hamilton Waldo, and who died in 1985. Among science fiction writers, there exists the coveted Theodore Sturgeon Memorial Award for best science fiction short story of the year, and the nominations director is David Truesdale who is editor of Tangent Sci-Fi review magazine. And I contacted him and he phoned John Ordover, Star Trek Books editor for Pocket Books, who bet his reputation on Theodore Sturgeon being the author of "Live long and prosper," which, of course is a phrase now licensed by Paramount Pictures for purposes of revenue generating T-shirts and collectible flotsam and jetsam and whatnot. But a broadcast journalist wants to be sure, and so I called Professor of Science Fiction writing Professor James Gunn at the University of Kansas in Lawrence whom, I was told, had an association with the late writer, and who put me in touch with Noel Sturgeon, Theodore Sturgeon's daughter, who confirms her father was the author of "Live long and prosper."

And I was satisfied as to having ascertained authorship of the universally familiar Vulcan aloha, until my search engine turned up an unexpected anomaly in the midst of Star Trek trivia: The Massachusetts state song.

It turns out that Massachusetts is unique among the fifty states possessed of the only Official State Song containing the Vulcan benediction. The second verse of "All Hail To Massachusetts" goes thusly: "All hail to grand old Bay State, the home of the bean and the cod, Where Pilgrims found a landing, and gave their thanks to God," written by Arthur J. Marsh, whose pairing of God with cod is unique in poetry, and the Vulcan greeting comes in the lines immediate following: "A land of opportunity in the good old USA, Where men *live long and prosper,* and people come to stay."

And, in that, prior to its official designation in 1981, All Hail to Massachusetts had been the unofficial state song since 1966, and was written previous to that, and in that Star Trek premiered in 1966, but the phrase did not appear until 1967, you'll allow as how Massachusetts's anthem composer Mr. Marsh appears to have an open and shut intellectual property claim against the Gene Roddenberry estate and Paramount Pictures. Sci-fi writer Sturgeon was raised in New York State and certainly was in the position to have been exposed to the Massachusetts State song and to have retained it subliminally.

And so, it is conceivable that, without Massachusetts, we would not possess the familiar phrase which is the Vulcan adios, in the same way that, without Massachusetts, we would also have no punch line for the one that goes, April Showers bring may flowers, and what do Mayflowers bring?"

Barbie Millicent Roberts, International Icon

In "Harvey," Elwood P. Dowd declares something like; "I've wrestled with reality for 35 years, doctor, and I'm happy to state I've finally won out over it," which I recalled when I was E-mailed the Barbie bio by a Barbie collector who desires me to mention that Barbie's 44th birthday is in March.

To many, Barbie is less an inanimate construction of mold-injected plastic, and more an international celebrity recognized as universally as Elvis by merely the mention of her first name.

And I called Barbie's people in El Segundo, California, who informed me that her actual birthday is March 9; a birth date she shares with Grandpa Walton (Will Greer), and Amerigo Vespucci. I spoke with Barbie P.R. assistant Cory Southwell, who, by virtue of her position, must believe in the reality of Barbie as earnestly as a Bishop does the Trinity. And I asked to be caught up on Barbie, inasmuch as I have not followed her life as closely as have those who maintain personal web sites about her. And this is the intelligence communicated to me.

Barbie's parents, George and Margaret Roberts, were married in San Francisco and named their first daughter

Barbie. Her middle name is Millicent, which will come as a surprise to those of us who were under the impression it was Trademark. They settled in Willows, Wisconsin, where Barbie went to Willows High School, which is where she met Ken, whose full name is Kenneth Carson. They have been dating since 1961, when, if she is now nearly 44, she was two. Parents George and Margaret were blessed with younger sister Skipper in 1964. Nearly thirty years later, Mrs. Roberts would give birth to Barbie's youngest siblings Stacey in 1992 and Kelly in 1995.

And, calculating that, if Barbie's mother was eighteen when Barbie was conceived in 1958, she would have been in her mid-fifties when Stacey and Kelly arrived. And, in that thirty years had elapsed since the birth of Skipper, we may assume her two most recent pregnancies were unplanned.

Skipper's first boyfriend was Scott in 1980, but not to the exclusion of others. She has also been seen in the company of Leonardo di Caprio. Ken was kept off the shelves during the late sixties and early 70s, so it is not clear what he was doing during the Vietnam War.

Some statistics. Two Barbies are sold every second. A little girl gets her first Barbie at age three and acquires six more before she is twelve. In Sweden, more Barbies have been sold than there are Swedes. 90% of serious Barbie collectors are forty-year-old women, and nearly half of them spend upwards of a thousand dollars a year. Also, if you placed the billion Barbies and family members ever sold, head to toe, they would circle the equator seven times. In her lifetime, Barbie has owned seventeen dogs, twelve horses, three ponies, five cats, a parrot, a chimpanzee, a panda, a lion cub, a seahorse, a giraffe and a zebra. She has worn clothes designed by Calvin Klein, Donna Karan, Oscar de la Renta, Nicole Miller, Christian Dior, Ann Klein, Ralph Lauren, Bill Blass and Gianni Versace and was presumably disconsolate about that whole Andrew Cunanan thing.

Barbie has signed a contract with Ferrari in which she will become a Formula One race driver, adding to her astounding resume Curriculum Vitae, in that she has been variously, in addition to a Rockette and an aerobics instructor; an astronaut, a paleontologist, an army medic in Desert Storm, a UNICEF diplomat, a Canadian Mountie, and an environmentalist, which she likely took up when it was discovered her molecular makeup is not carbon-based, but rather, polyvinyl chloride.

As a result, Barbie has tested PVC positive. But, as she is in a monogamous relationship with Ken, who is also PVC positive, there is no impediment to a normal loving relationship insofar as transmission is unlikely between consenting individuals with no genitalia.

Hair on the Soap

I visited the grocery store yesterday, where I made my periodic inspection to ascertain the present state of play-enhancing bathtub kid's soaps. And I regret to report that in this epoch of technological advancement of unparalleled velocity, we don't hold a candle to our 1960s supremacy in the area of basic steel manufacturing and recreational bathtub soaps. To be sure, one can obtain, this very day, a Mr. Bubble container whose bottle is a raft and whose cap is a Mr.

Bubble squirting squeeze toy. And girls may enjoy the luxury of Barbie Bubble Bath, whose label is also in French where we learn that Bubble Bath is Bain Mousse. And there remains a spark of originality in Sesame Street Finger Paint Bubble Bath, with which, one may draw on bathtub walls before scrubbing one's graffiti into foam. But at no time in hygiene history was this nation richer in rub-a-dub-dubbing options than in the period from the Kennedy through the Nixon administrations.

   The first generation of Americans that had grown up with Silly Putty were accustomed to products bearing the names Silly and Crazy and Wacky. And thus it was that we embraced Crazy Foam and Silly Soap. Crazy Foam was soap shot from an aerosol can like shave cream and the commercials encouraged us to decorate ourselves with mustaches and beards and sideburns. The cans were meant to be characters, and if the character was a duck the foam would dispense from a projecting plastic beak, and so forth. And there was Silly Soap, upon which appeared cartoon characters and bearing messages such as, Woo-woo the Whale says, "Silly Soap Makes Bathing Fun," which we accepted, being of the opinion Woo-woo wouldn't have said it if it were not so. Between Crazy Foam and Silly Soap, children of the sixties emptied sufficient aerosol canisters at tub time to deplete the ozone layer for a generation, minimum. And for those of us who went through cans of the stuff by the gross, it will break a man's heart to see that a collector will pay 80 dollars for an empty container of Superman Crazy Foam.

And there were Soakies; bubble bath in plastic containers shaped like cartoon characters or monsters bearing the maxim, "Soaky Soaks You Clean and Leaves No Bathtub Ring," offering the labor-saving promise of a wash-cloth-free bath involving no actual exertion of effort. And there was a Smokey the Bear Soaky and a Porky Pig Soaky, the first in a series of bubble-bath containers molded in the likenesses of everybody from Quickdraw McGraw's little buddy Babalooey to Doggy Daddy's boy Augie Doggie. And, despite tender years, what child was flim-flammed by the jingle which went: "Soaky soaks you clean in oceans full of fun, scrubbly-bubbly, flibbity-flubbity clean before you're done. Soaky soaks you clean and every girl and boy gets a toy when it's empty, when it's empty it's a toy," as American youth, even pre-Tet Offensive, was sophisticated enough to distinguish an empty soap container from a toy.

And Dial Soap had something called Soaprize, which was a floating bar of soap with a picture on the outside of the toy hidden inside once the soap was all rubbed away, such as Sylvester the Submarine or Alvin the Alligator.

But, by far and away the winner in the category of ancient tub soap your kids will insist you entirely made up, was the Fuzzy Wuzzy. Fuzzy Wuzzys were soap animals that grew hair. The soap bear, or monkey, or tiger, was packaged in a box resembling a circus train car with the words, "I Grow Fur," above the barred window. One would lather up with a Fuzzy Wuzzy, and was then directed to place it for some time in a dark place, during which a luxurious coat of thick mold would magically appear. The effect was not as appealing as it sounds. But to discourage moms from throwing the repellant object away, it contained a hidden toy in its center to ensure continued use. And I went to eBay to seek out a Fuzzy Wuzzy and happened upon the final 8 minutes of a bidding war in progress, in which electronic pseudonym dr.tomorrow bested Internet AKA play2together to the tune of 86 dollars, a considerable premium on the asking price of 19. The description declares this Fuzzy Wuzzy resides in its original box, slightly worn from sitting on the shelf in an old shuttered drug store since 1967. And I entertained the desire to swoop in out of the sun unseen and undetected to snatch the item from the grasp of the competing bidders for the five seconds it took for me to hear, in my mind, my wife's inquisition voice requesting confirmation that I had paid 90 dollars for a bar of soap with hair on it.

Chapter 4—History and Other Myths

Why the Maya Left Town

There has been a lot of academic speculation and scholarly supposition offering puffed-up conjectures as to the causes of the abandonment of the ancient Mayan Cities such as Chichen Itza and Tulum and Palenque and Tikal and all the rest.

And many people mistakenly believe that the Maya vanished without a trace when, in fact, they are alive and well and making tequila sunrises and turning down beds at the all-inclusives all along the Caribbean coast from Cancun south. The Maya remained in the Yucatan through the conquest of the Spaniards and remain the indigenous populations of portions of Mexico, Belize, and Guatemala, but it is undeniable that they mysteriously left their ancient cities to be enveloped by the lush foliage of impenetrable forests and I'm here to tell you why.

Although one might characterize me as an armchair authority; what began, early on, as a presumption, developed into a sneaking suspicion, which grew to become a vague notion and evolved into a hazy idea, which I will set forth here as a full blown shot in the dark. I have read the works of many of the leading Maya scholars, including Michael Coe's "Breaking the Mayan Code" in which he cites breakthroughs in the translations of the Mayan picture writing visible on the ziggurats, or stepped pyramids, which characterize meso-American monumental architecture. Coe is a Harvard-trained curator of anthropology at the Peabody Museum at Yale, who cites the work of Yale Maya scholar David Joralemon, whose paper on Mayan blood sacrifice, quoting, "described how the classic rulers of Mayan cities, assisted by their wives, would regularly perforate their penises with horrific, deified bloodletters fashioned from stingray spines." Unquote. On significant religious occasions the elite among males would pierce his penis with the spine of a stringray, and pull the spine through the penis and collect the resulting blood for a rite of sanctification.

Other Mayan inscriptions tell of the use of the stingray spine to pierce the tongue as well to produce blood for a divine offering. Scholars, too, have deciphered enough of the heiroglyphs relating to the Mayan's sacred ball games to know that the game of pok-ta-pok was like a theologically-themed round of hacky-sack. Players wore pads on their elbows, knees and ankles and the object of the game was to deflect a hard rubber ball the size of a baseball off the pads and a girdle worn around the waist, into stone rings on the walls of the ball court. One school of thought holds that the winner of such an event was sacrificed, either beheaded or his living heart cut from his body. A contrary view is that it was the loser who was sacrificed.

Other customs included the removal of a virgin's heart on the elevated altar of a Mayan pyramid by priests to win the favor of the gods, and the drowning of virgins in the sacred pool to a similar purpose. Recent evidence has emerged suggesting the presence of ritualized cannibalism; the sacramental consuming of sacrificed human meat, cooked with corn.

And I believe it does not take a great leap of faith to suggest that the Mayas left their cities to the leafy tendrils of jungle flora because they'd had it with this baloney. I see a generation of Mayan youth, questioning authority, as is the nature of youth, saying no, when the question was whether they wanted to play ball. Saying no, when the opportunity presented itself to assume political office requiring ritual penis perforation. Saying no, when asked whether one wished to have an enemy for dinner. And saying yes to losing one's virginity at one's earliest opportunity.

It was just a more enlightened Mayan youth looking to leave the older generation to their stingray spines and heart-ripping and head-hacking and bloodletting, who set out from the big stone cities in search of a place where people could keep all the blood inside their bodies where it belonged. I say it was a new generation of Maya declining to become their father's Maya. They rebelled against their parents' customs just as many of us couldn't wait to flee the house of our own bridge-playing parents who played the Ray Conniff Singers

S'Wonderful album over and over and sang the Yellow Rose of Texas along with Mitch Miller and suspended fruit and mayonnaise in Jell-o molds.

The Assassination of Andrew Jackson

Even though it is usual for me to read, almost daily, of the incorrectness of some fact I have unnecessarily carried around in my head since high school, such as that Rangoon is the capitol of Burma, I was nevertheless surprised to read that it turns out Andrew Jackson was assassinated.

Doctors at Northeastern Ohio University College of Medicine, whose day-planners were apparently uncluttered, decided to run tests on hair clipped from the seventh president, and expected to find high levels of mercury, which Jackson's doctors prescribed to him, as was the custom of the day, for his severe constipation, which I shall try not to be reminded of when I encounter his portrait on a 20 dollar bill. It was known Jackson had severe mood swings and irritability and paranoia and it was unknown to doctors that ingestion of mercury could result in a lengthy tour of the cracker factory. But despite the levels of mercury in his medicine, Jackson's hair samples showed it was not excessive mercury but rather lead, which contributed to his deteriorating health in the years leading to his death. And how the lead got there is a story.

Andrew Jackson had a race horse named Truxton which made him tens of thousands of dollars but, after a race which didn't happen when the challenging horse pulled up lame, a friend of Jackson insinuated some irregularity in the manner in which another man handled a bet with Jackson over the forfeited race. And the slandered man's son-in-law, Charles Dickinson, commenced to feuding with Andrew Jackson's friend and Andrew Jackson got between them, which is always a bad idea. So Dickinson started fighting with Andrew Jackson instead, and, in that he was a crack shot, he tried to goad Jackson into gunplay and called him names like "equivocator," which Jackson ignored until Dickinson published a statement in the newspaper calling Jackson a "poltroon," at which Jackson challenged him to a duel in that he was tired of having to look words up in the dictionary. And Dickinson chose pistols and fired first and the lead bullet broke two of Jackson's ribs and stopped two inches from his heart, and then Jackson, clutching his chest, aimed slowly and shot Dickinson dead on the spot.

That was in 1806. In 1813, Andrew Jackson officiated at the duel of two other men which resulted in one of them, Jesse Benton, receiving a bullet through both buttock cheeks, eliciting a certain amount of ridicule, and the wounded man's brother, future senator Thomas Hart Benton, castigated Jackson for his part in it and Jackson told Benton he'd horsewhip him. And this debate escalated into gunfire, and the Benton brothers shot Jackson in the arm and he carried that bullet for nearly twenty years. And doctors now think the lead leaching into his blood from these bullets caused lead colic resulting in severe abdominal cramps and intestinal problems; causing his teeth to fall out and declining health leading to eventual death. And so it would seem Charles Dickinson fatally wounded Andrew Jackson in

1806 but was not charged, being dead; and the Benton brothers fatally wounded Andrew Jackson again in 1813 but got away with it in that Jackson took 32 years to die.

And this story moved me to call the foremost expert on Andrew Jackson in this country, Robert Remini, emeritus professor of history at the University of Illinois at Chicago, who has written extensively on Andrew Jackson and I asked him what he thought of the 1953 Charlton Heston movie, *The President's Lady* which was about Mrs. Andrew Jackson, and he allowed as how he thought Susan Hayward was fine in the role. And he reminded me there was another time when Andrew Jackson fought a duel but that one ended with him and his opponent ducking behind trees while shooting at each other until they called a truce.

And on the one hand one must question the wisdom of electing a chief of state who habitually and voluntarily attracts small arms fire, while on the other hand it can be said that, although a lawyer, he chose to settle his disputes without one. And whereas Andrew Jackson was known to be an indifferent speller, who was known to spell the same word three different ways in a single letter, I am fond of his response to a critic, that, "It's a mighty poor mind that can only think of one way to spell a word."

Where did that Monkey Chase that Weasel?

I received the following communication from E-mailer Kerry Seghers. "While being forced to listen to the ice cream truck play 'Pop! Goes the Weasel,' over and over, my neighbor and I got into a debate. I grew up singing, 'round and round the carpenter's bench, the monkey chased the weasel.' My neighbor insists the words are 'all around the mulberry bush, the monkey chased the weasel.' I argue that the odds of a monkey, weasel, and mulberry bush all being located in the same region are slim, whereas a carpenter could very well keep a monkey and a weasel, which could, in theory, chase each other around the work bench, although most work benches are situated against a wall, mitigating against chasing 'round them." And like Mr. Segher's neighbor, when I was knee-high to a duck, when mention was made of weasel-chasing I understood it to be taking place all around the mulberry bush.

And so I thought to ascertain the correct identity of the object encircled; in the event I had been deluded since childhood into mistaking a bench for a bush. And as far as I can tell, a man named William McNeil has spent more time researching this subject than seems at all necessary, for a treatise he wrote entitled *The Long History of Pop Goes the Weasel*. I reached Mr. McNeil at his home in North Carolina where he was convalescing from a cardiac event and he's feeling much better now thanks. He traces the genealogy of the Weasel Song to early 17th century England, where it was a child's singing game, carried to the New World in 1620 by the Puritan people who later became the punchline to the one that goes, "April showers bring May flowers. And what do Mayflowers bring?"

In the eighteenth century the tune became popular with fiddlers, and overspread the expanding nation with performers amending the lyrics as they pleased. The tune was published, mainly without lyrics, in 1853, in several locations here and in England. The earliest printed version of the song was in an 1858 anthology entitled *100 Comic Songs*, edited by J.W. Turner, in which it was declared that "All around the cobbler's house, The Monkey chased the people, And after them in double haste, Pop went the weasel."

And it becomes apparent that a Weasel in this context was not a varmint but a euphemism. A weasel was a tool used by cobblers and hatters and tailors and could be converted to ready money at a pawnshop where it would be hocked, or "popped." An 1853 version was attributed variously to T.C. Andrews, Charles Twiggs, and (by the Oxford Dictionary of Quotations and Bartlett's Familiar Quotations) W.R. Mandale, whose verse "Up and down the City Road, In and out the Eagle, That's the way the money goes, Pop goes the weasel," described extracting money from the pawn shop so as to finance a trip up London's City Road to the Eagle tavern. Of the contested initial verse, the one about the carpenter's bench appears to predate the mulberry bush (which is any of a variety of flowering raspberries), although carpenter's bench was, itself, predated by cobbler's bench, which was predated by cobbler's house. But even Bill McNeil, the world's foremost authority on *Pop Goes The Weasel*, confessed that he'll be hanged if he knows the meaning of the monkey.

Oh, and it is not the Incy-Wincy Spider. It is the Itsy Bitsy Spider and the hand movement it is thumb to middle finger, not index finger. And Dr. Phillip Hiscock, professor of folklore and popular culture at the Memorial University of Newfoundland, the world's foremost authority on *Ring-Around The Rosie*, says he doesn't care who told you, it has nothing to do with the 14th century London plague called the Black Death. Somebody made that up and it was repeated to the degree that everybody came to believe it. The very first published version was the 1881 Mother Goose one which goes, "Ring-a-ring o' roses, A pocket full of posies, Hush! Hush! Hush! Hush! We're all tumbled down." He figures generations of babies pronounced the hushes as ashes and the parents mimicked the baby-talk because it was adorable. Also, for those who are bothered by the part in *Hickory Dickory Dock* when "The clock struck one, The mouse ran down…" because it doesn't rhyme; some do-gooder corrected the grammar at the expense of the rhyme, which is properly rendered, "The clock struck one, And down he run." And after the people always *shout John Jacob Jingleheimer Schmidt*, it is not Tra-la-la-la-la-la-la. It is Da-da-da-da-da-da-da. You're welcome.

A Lusty Lothario was our 16th President

In 1865, Abraham Lincoln died from a bullet wound to the brain at 7:22 in the morning on the 15th of April, commencing his ascension to penny-profile sainthood. In the ensuing six score and eighteen years, the search for the flesh-and-blood Lincoln has been thwarted by protective biographers to the degree many were willing to suspend disbelief at the theory, propounded two years ago by gay playwright Larry Kramer, that Lincoln carried on a homosexual relationship with his best friend Joshua Speed. Kramer has claimed to have seen pages of a secret diary written by Joshua Speed, found beneath floorboards of the Springfield store, above which, the two men shared the same bed for four years, though scholars have seen nothing of these documents.

Now, new evidence has arisen, suggesting that, much to the contrary, Lincoln was instead a lady-killer, a lover-boy, a hormone-driven devotee of the cult of Aphrodite. In an article in the Atlantic Monthly Lincoln scholar Douglas Wilson, director of Lincoln studies at Knox College in Galesburg, reveals the existence of two secret notebooks in which details of Lincoln's private life were compiled by his law partner William Herndon, who became his biographer following the assassination. Herndon referred to one of the secret notebooks in a letter in which he writes, quoting, "About the year 1835, Mr. Lincoln went to Beardstown, and, during a devilish passion, had connection with a girl and caught the syphilis. Lincoln told me of this, and, in a moment of folly, I made a note of it in a little memorandum book," which he complained of lending to an acquaintance of Lincoln who would not give it back. Herndon made no mention of these long-lost confidential notebooks in his official biographical writings, but historian Wilson reports that the year following the assassination, Herdon entertained a house guest; women's' rights activist and journalist Caroline Healey Dall, and permitted her to peruse what one might characterize as his secret Lincoln logs.

Now, letters and journal-entries written by Ms. Dall have been uncovered by a literary scholar at the Bryn Mawr College library, to which they were donated by her descendants, and they suggest the skirt-chasing Lincoln-Lothario scenario. Shocked by the Herndon notebook material in 1866, Ms. Dall cancelled a planned public lecture on Lincoln's virtue, and wrote, quoting, "Among the papers I examined, are affidavits from prostitutes, prize fighters, and the very lowest human beings of all sorts. (Mr.) Herndon's object in gathering these together has been to show Lincoln's essential integrity, in even the foulest circumstances of his life; but—Good Heavens—rather than publish these, I would rather allow it (his integrity) to be doubted." Historian Wilson relates that her notes suggest Lincoln was unchaste before marriage and unfaithful afterward, as she wrote, "All the lawyers on circuit, and more dissolute women than I could count, know A.L.'s profligacy, as regards women, to be greater than is common to married men, even here," and continues, "I remember that when I read Aristophanes, I was thankful that there were vices for which the English language has no name," to which she adds, with disgust; "I had not been in Springfield then."

And thus Caroline Healy Dall paints a lusty Lincoln portrait of our 16th president as a manly emancipator who ironically was a slave to his vice, whose name, like that of his vice president, was Johnson.

One of the revelations in the Dall diaries is that she had seen papers that Lincoln had retained lawyers to discover the identity of his real father, in that he had long suspected that his own mother Nancy Hanks was illegitimate, and that Thomas Lincoln married her when she was already pregnant. His intention, writes Ms. Dall, was not to enter the White House as a Lincoln if his legal right to his real name could be established. The investigation suggested, but did not prove, that his natural father was likely a more educated man than the illiterate Thomas Lincoln, by the name of Bloomfield. Which of course moves us to wonder all the more how subsequent events might have been different were Illinoisans required by statute to affix a license plate bearing the motto, "Land of Bloomfield," to their Bloomfield Town Cars.

And Saddam Hussein Loves Whitney Houston

I consider myself among that demographic of individuals who do not like Nazis and who do like the classical music of Richard Wagner, who, this being America, I like to call Dick Wagner.

Dick Wagner's music was a favorite of Adolph Hitler, which is why the Simon Weisenthal Center asked the Supreme Court of Israel to stop Daniel Barenboim from playing, at the Israeli Music Festival, a Wagner piece from the Opera, *Die Walkure*, which they allege is anti-Israeli. Barenboim, an Israeli, was of a contrary view; a view that this piece has earned its classification as a classical classic. And Barenboim went ahead and conducted a Wagner piece and I seem to recollect it was from *The Valkyrie*; the rousing *Ride of the Valkyries* which movie-goers will remember from the helicopter gunship Vietnam War scenes in *Apocalypse Now*. Which is part of Dick Wagner's four operas *The Ring of the Nibelung*, based on the ancient Scandinavian and Germanic conception of the world as manifested in the Gods of Valhalla, the realm of men, and the dark realm of the Nibelungs, dwarves, and leave me not neglect the Giants and Norns. It is about heroism and love and incest and dragon slaying. Most recently Barenboim staged a Wagner marathon at the Berlin State Opera, conducting all ten Wagner operas.

And if it is true that Hitler said "anyone who wants to understand National Socialism should just listen to Wagner," his saying it doesn't make it so. Charles Manson liked the Beatles. *The White Album*, in particular. Does this condemn us to have no truck with Rocky Raccoon; to scrupulously avoid the Blackbird singing in the dead of night; to renounce Revolution; to forswear Ob-La-Di-ing? Before they turned the valve on Timothy McVeigh, he submitted as his last statement the William Ernest Henley poem that goes, "Out of the night that covers me, Black as the pit from pole to pole, I thank whatever gods may be, For my unconquerable soul." And after more verses it concludes, "It matters not how strait the gate, How charged with punishments the scroll. I am the master of my fate. I am the captain of my soul." Which in no way should tar Mr. Henley with the McVeigh brush. A while back, Anita and I went to the symphony, where, by chance, baton-bobbing Barenboim conducted three movements by Wagner, including a piece called the Idyll from *Seigfried*, which is one of the Ring operas in which Seigfried gives the magic ring, as a token of his love, to Brunnhilde, who is the character most people think of when one hears, "It's not over till the fat lady sings." And it turns out that this particular piece was, for years, a private piece of music composed by Dick Wagner as a birthday present for Mrs. Wagner on Christmas Day in 1870, 19 years before Adolph Hitler was born. Wagner needed a pastorale for Siegfried and the Mrs. agreed to donate their song.

And therein lies a convoluted and sexy tale. Dick Wagner and Franz Liszt were pals and Wagner dedicated an opera to Liszt and Liszt dedicated a symphony to Wagner, and we find them as bosom buddies when Wagner first meets Liszt's daughter Cosima at dinner in Paris when he is forty and she is fifteen. He is infatuated with her but is married and when she is 19 she marries her father's piano protégé Hans von Bulow, and the bride and groom honeymoon at the Wagner's house whereupon Dick experiences urges. Franz Liszt isn't blind and, as Dick and Cosima's relationship heats up, Liszt's friendship with Wagner cools. Finally, when he is age 50 and she is 25, Dick and Cosima profess their love for each other with sobs and tears and begin an adulterous affair. And they have a baby, at which Cosima leaves von Bulow to live with Wagner and to become his second wife, his first having expired. And Hans von Bulow went on to a distinguished career as a concert pianist and a conductor and ancestor to Claus von Bulow, who was portrayed by Jeremy Irons in Reversal of Fortune, with Ron Silver as Alan Dershowitz. Claus von Bulow and Sunny von Bulow had a daughter, and they named her Cosima, after her scandalous namesake; Dick Wagner's lover and Hans Von Bulow's ex and Franz Liszt's daughter. By the way, Sunny von Bulow continues, after twenty years and counting, to vegetate comatosely in a private hospital in New York, while Claus remains close with daughter Cosima, which is understandable, in that she inherited, with her half-brother and sister, 150 million dollars. Anyhow, I'm with Maestro Barenboim. It's okay to hate Nazis and like Wagner. And Volkswagens.

The War Between the States' Songs

The state of Maryland is again considering replacing its official state song, which is "Maryland, My Maryland," because it calls Abraham Lincoln a despot and the northern states scum.

And it turns out that the Maryland state song was written by a teacher in Louisiana who was from Maryland and became riled and wrathful at reading about how Union troops from Massachusetts were marching through Baltimore in 1861 when a secessionist mob attacked them and some rioters were killed. And James Ryder Randall wrote a poem and it was put to the tune of "Oh, Tannenbaum." And the whole first verse goes, "The despot's heel is on thy shore, Maryland, my Maryland. His torch is at thy temple door, Maryland, my Maryland. Avenge the patriotic gore. That flecked the streets of Baltimore, And be the battle-queen of yore, Maryland, my Maryland." And it continues spewing for eleven verses, citing obscure historical figures in verses such as "Remember Carroll's sacred trust, Remember Howard's warlike thrust…." And "With Ringgold's spirit for the fray, With Watson's blood at Monterey, With fearless Lowe and dashing May, Maryland, my Maryland." And I called the Maryland State House to ask Representative Peter Franchot, who sponsored the last challenge to the state song, if he remembered Carroll and Howard and Ringgold and Watson and May and he allowed as how he did not. And the final verse goes, "I hear the distant thunder-hum, Maryland, my Maryland. The Old Line bugle, fife and drum, Maryland, my Maryland. She is not dead, nor deaf nor dumb. Huzza! She spurns the northern scum! She breathes! She burns! She'll come! She'll come! Maryland, etcetera."

And the fact of the matter is that the Civil War rages on in the Official Songs of the South. The South Carolina state song, written by Henry Timrod in 1862, also picks a beef with Abraham Lincoln as it starts out, "The despot treads thy sacred sands, Thy pines give shelter to his bands, Thy sons stand by with idle hands, Carolina," and at its conclusion it is a call to arms as it goes, "Fling down the gauntlet to the Huns, And roar the challenge from thy guns; Then leave the future to thy sons, Carolina!" Yankees are Huns in South Carolina; scum in Maryland.

Other southern states official songs don't officially hate the north, but have their own particular vulnerabilities peculiar to the period, such as Florida's, in which Stephen Foster wrote, "All de world am sad and dreary, Eb-rywhere I roam' Oh, Darkeys, how my heart grows weary, Far from de old folks at home!" Or Kentucky's in which Stephen Foster wrote, "Oh the head must bow and the back will have to bend, Wherever the darkey may go. A few more days and the trouble all will end, In the field where the sugar-canes may grow." And Kentucky sanitized the word darkeys to read "people" a few years back. And then there is Virginia's which goes, "There's where I labored so hard for old massa, Day after day in the field of yellow corn, No place on earth do I love more sincerely, Than old Virginny, the state where I was born."

And I scanned the state songs of the northern states to discover lyrics of a more mawkish and maudlin mix such as "And tho' we seek far and wide, Our search will be in vain, To find a fairer spot on earth, Than Maine! Maine! Maine!", or, also to the tune of "Oh Tannenbaum," "I sing a State of all the best, Michigan, my Michigan; I sing a State with riches blest, Michigan, my Michigan." And absent from the state songs of the north are belligerent bombast from the 1860s, save for Illinois, which, likewise, perpetuates the feud, and by way of example: "When the southern host withdrew, Pitting Grey against the Blue, there were none more brave than you, Illinois, Illinois." And I think it is high time to get over it and follow the example of West Virginia, which has seven official state songs, or Ohio, whose legislature passed the following resolution in November of 1985, on behalf of those bored with smarmy "Beautiful Ohio." Quoting from the Ohio Revised Code: "Whereas, Adoption of this resolution will not take too long, cost the state anything, or affect the quality of life in this state to any appreciable degree, and if we in the legislature just go ahead and pass the darn thing, we can get on with more important stuff; and Whereas, Sloopy lives in a very bad part of town, and everybody, yeah, tries to put my Sloopy down; and Whereas, Sloopy, I don't care what your daddy do, 'cause you know Sloopy girl, I'm in love with you: therefore be it resolved, That we, the members of the 116th General Assembly of Ohio, in adopting this Resolution, name "Hang on Sloopy" as the official rock song of the State of Ohio."

So Maryland would be well advised to dump the confederate sore-loser scum song and go with the product of a more contemporary local. Mama Cass was from there. On occasions of state they'd be dancing in the streets.

Flatulence in Western Culture

I see by my desk calendar that Lawsuit Abuse Awareness Week falls annually in late September, and by way of example the calendar cites the taxpayer cost of defending the state from a prison inmate who sued Michigan, holding prison food responsible for his chronic and sometimes painful flatulence, and I would challenge the characterization of this lawsuit as frivolous.

The expulsion of an excessive accumulation of air in the digestive tract is no joke to those suddenly and involuntarily afflicted in our nation's elevators, funeral homes, and symphony halls. Humankind's attempt to grapple with this problem spans history, from Pythagoras (who, in addition to contemplating the hypotenuse of a right triangle also warned his followers to eschew beans as digestive mischief-makers) to Adolph Hitler, whose physicians prescribed a vegetarian diet to ameliorate his chronic flatulence and abdominal cramping.

I phoned Dr. Anatoly Liberman, a Scandinavian and Germanic scholar and expert in medieval custom at the University of Minnesota in Minneapolis, who says that in ancient times behaviors such as nose-blowing, belching, and wind-breaking were unrestricted by polite constraint. And he tells of a renowned Norwegian archer-warrior known to history as Einarr Pambarskelfir, who was asleep in the great hall when his adversaries came upon him and one took a piece of straw and tickled his nose with it, at which point the sleeping archer "cut the Jarlsberg," as it were, and awakened to taunting merriment and shouts bestowing upon him the nickname, the rough translation of which would be, "super-gas-passer," at which, in a rage, he put an end to their laughing by slaying them all. Dr. Liberman adds that, in medieval Germany, those who were bashful about passing gas were considered weak or effeminate, and in German the word "pimpf" is derisively applied to those who can't produce a good "pumpf." By the end of the 16th century, Shakespearean-era jesters amused the royal court with imitations of forcefully expelled intestinal gasses to much applause. In the 1890s, we read that one of the most popular stars of the French stage, Le Petomane, acquired considerable wealth by playing tunes, extinguishing candles, and imitating bird calls with the gas expelled from his person as he trod the boards at the Moulin Rouge.

In that the process is biologically natural and universal, the stifling of it is a relatively recent social convention. As recently as 1879, the Etymological Dictionary of the English Language, published by Oxford University, defined flatulence as the quality of being windy, as in, "It's flatulent outside. Good kite-flying weather." From the Latin: flatus; meaning "blowing, or a breath," which has come to mean the breath of hydrogen produced by bacteria breaking down undigested material in the large intestine; with the odor of hydrogen sulfide the byproduct. And even though researchers have measured human gas output between a pint and a half gallon per day, and the frequency of gas passing in healthy adult males in the neighborhood of thirteen passages daily, in modern society, of course, the only desirable windbreaker has London Fog on the inside label, whereas the f--t word is rarely used in polite intercourse; the American Greeting Card industry notwithstanding.

Corporate nutrition consultant Matt O'Neill is promoting a campaign to persuade people to pass gas to promote good health. His slogan is, "Better an empty house than a bad tenant." But most consider the behavior unacceptable, like Wendy Guthrie of Mooresville, Indiana, who recounts on the web site of the Center for Science in the Public Interest that the result of her family's horrific introduction to barbecue-flavored Wow chips with Olestra was, in her words, "extreme urgency accompanied by uncontrollable flatulence."

The subject then, is serious, and not frivolous, or a joke, although there is the joke about the World Health Organization nurse visiting a medical clinic in rural Mazabuka, fifty miles outside Lusaka, in Zambia, who overhears one local village doctor insist to another, "I'm telling you it's wumba, W-U-M-B-A," to which the second doctor disagrees, "No, it's woombaa, W-O-O-M-B-A-A," and the first disputes, "No, wumba." At which the nurse interrupts to interject, "I believe you will find, Gentlemen, that it is womb, W-O-M-B." To which the doctors are momentarily silent until one of them retorts, "Madam, I doubt that you have ever SEEN a water buffalo, let alone heard one pass gas in a mud bog."

Santa Anna's Leg

I was watching an old episode of the fine animated cartoon program King of the Hill, and the story was about Santa Anna's leg, and at the very end, over the closing credits, the voice of politically conservative Texas cartoon character Hank Hill was heard declaring that the real artificial leg of Santa Anna resides in an Illinois museum and if viewers wanted it returned to the people of Mexico they should contact the United States Senator from Illinois.

And this piqued my curiosity and I undertook to ascertain whether the story, as set forth by King of the Hill is historically accurate or a farcical fabrication; and these are the facts as I have researched them: A. We have the leg. B. We're keeping it.

The story begins in March of 1836. The Alamo. Four thousand of Mexican military strongman Generalissimo Antonio Lopez de Santa Anna's infantry, artillery, and cavalry surround 189 brave Texians, and in the siege which ends on March 6, slaughter them to the last man. Forty-six days later. April 21st. The Generalissimo is having sport in his tent with a beautiful mulatto indentured servant Texian girl, Emily West, who (it later turned out) volunteered to use sex as a weapon to divert Santa Anna, while the forces of Sam Houston surprised the superior Mexican forces and routed them in eighteen minutes before the Mexican general could react, with a loss of only nine Texians. And Emily West is widely believed to be the woman about whom they wrote the Yellow Rose of Texas.

Anyhow, Santa Anna was captured the next day and he traded Texas for a ticket home, and so he was freed to fight again another day. And he defeated the French invaders at Vera Cruz two years later and the lower half of his left leg was shot off and he paraded the leg through Mexico City and had a state funeral for it and obtained an artificial leg made out of cork and covered with leather, which he bought for thirteen hundred dollars from a New York legmaker. And then President Polk declared war on Mexico to win the land west of Texas so as to fill up the whole map, from sea to shining sea, with the USA, and the Mexican-American War resulted in Manifest Destiny becoming the correct answer on the midterms.

And during this war, on April 18, 1847, while nearby raged the battle of Cerro Gordo, near Veracruz, the Generalissimo was relaxing in his carriage with a lunch of roast chicken when he was surprised by the men of the Illinois Volunteer Infantry, Fourth Regiment, and Santa Anna leaped on his horse and escaped, leaving the Illinois soldiers to eat his chicken and steal his leg. And so they carried it home with them to Illinois as a war trophy, and they showed it around and then gave it to the Illinois State Military Museum and it resides, at this very moment, displayed in a glass case in the hall outside the office of the Adjutant General at the headquarters of the Illinois National Guard on the corner of North Grand and MacArthur in Springfield. And further research reveals that the writers of King of the Hill incorrectly directed viewers to request the leg's return to Mexico of the Senator from Illinois, because it turns out Santa Anna's leg is the property of the State of

Illinois and none of the federal government's business. And so the fact of the matter is that only the Governor of the State of Illinois has the power to return Santa Anna's leg to Mexico.

And when I contacted the governor's office, I was informed that, since Mexico hasn't asked for it back, there would appear to be no urgency in pursuing the matter. And it turns out that Santa Anna's real left leg was stolen from its tomb in Mexico and never found, so the left leg left in Springfield is the only left leg left.

Maternal Issues make Maui One Twisted God

I was planning a trip to Hawaii. And since my knowledge of the history of Hawaii is limited to facts such as that, on Magnum P.I., the voice of the unseen Robin Masters was that of Orson Welles (until his death in 1985 by virtue of being the size of a small utility vehicle), I went to Borders and picked up a book entitled *Hawaii*, by James Michener.

And when I began to read, it occurred to me that I had forgotten that James Michener always commences his novels in a historical period just after the Big Bang, and just before the volcanic cones rising from the sea-bottom actually break the surface, and there is little character development until the evolution of single-celled organisms. And so I shelved the big fat book and obtained a thin book all about Hawaiian mythology.

And just listen to this: Long ago, Ku, the god of war and the sunrise, was the absolute top dog god. And he was married to Hina, the Earth mother, who had dominion over reproduction and whose job title also included Goddess of Women's Work. And it turned out that she had a love affair with Kane, the god of woodsmen, and as a result gave birth to the first man. And this was not the last affair she had, as the literature paints her as quite promiscuous. And we read that she was out looking for seaweed one day, and she found a man's loincloth on the beach, and she put it on, which caused her to become pregnant; and she fell into a deep sleep and when she awoke she gave birth to Maui. This is all in the book.

And Maui was a trickster, and was perpetually doing things daring and prankish. He stole the fire from the mud hens while they were roasting bananas, and lassoed the sun to slow it down so there would be more sunshine. And, according to this book, the way he did this was to lasso the sun god's genitals with a rope woven from his sister's pubic hair, and the sun begged him to take it easy, as the sun would do anything if Maui just stopped pulling on that rope. And the sun god made a deal to slow down, and more sunlight gave Maui more time to fish. And as he was fishing one day, Maui caught a huge fish and was fighting to reel in this fish, and as he battled it the fish turned into land. And his line broke and the land turned into the Hawaiian Islands, which would have been connected were Maui able to pull the fish all the way out of the water before the line broke.

Also, way back, the sky rested on the Earth, and the plants and bushes tried to push the sky up, but it was too heavy, and so Maui pushed the sky up; first to the treetops, and then he clean-and-jerked it over the mountaintops where it remains today.

And Maui's final prank came when he encountered Hina, his mother, sleeping on the ground. And he decided it would be a great joke were he to crawl back inside her womb. But, as he tried it, he got stuck halfway in, with his legs and feet dangling outside. And the birds who were his pals began to laugh at his predicament and the laughing awakened Hina, who was not amused and proceeded to squeeze Maui to death.

Which is a fine story in the public domain which Disney might consider assigning Pixar to bring to the screen by Christmas with some great new Tim Rice and Alan Mencken tunes. And one will agree that these traditional Hawaiian native beliefs provide strong evidence that the ancient Polynesians were not unfamiliar with controlled substances. (Note: 15 years after this monologue, Disney premiered *Moana*).

The Tissue Issue in Toilet History

Since it is well known in the broadcasting industry that, as a result of the Federal Courts having upheld the prohibition by Congress of broadcasting—during the hours of 6am through 10pm---material which depicts or describes in terms patently offensive as measured by contemporary community standards, sexual or excretory organs or activities; I must tread carefully as I describe, in some detail, man's excretory history, which I learned about after reading that, of all nations in the European Union, Britain has the costliest toilet paper. It turns out that Andrex toilet paper, now owned by Kimberly Clark, has, for fifty years, set such a luxurious standard for toilet paper that the British consumer will abide no less.

For a standard pack of four rolls, the British pay twice as much as the Germans and the French, and two and a half times as much as Americans, because, compared with the American and European rolls, British toilet paper is four grams heavier per square meter and 2 millimeters wider. And rather than the U.S. color-of-choice; white--- the British consumer selects from Summer Peach, Meadow Green, Breeze Blue, Honeysuckle, Magnolia, and a palette of 45 other hues, as the British homeowner requires the paper to exactly match bathroom décor.

Which is illustrative of the high state of British civilization, in that toilet historians declare the rise of civilized society and toilet technology have advanced together in lockstep. To learn more, I phoned R.M.P. Sinha, the director of the Museum of Toilets in New Delhi, India, whose parent company operates three thousand pay-per-use public toilets in India, and who pointed me to his toilet history web site, where the sitting toilet in India may be traced back to 25 hundred BC.

Roman Emperor Vespasian levied a tax on indoor toilets, and Roman society would urinate in full view in silver urination pots held by slaves while continuing to eat and drink. In Hindu scripture it is considered saintly not to defecate at all, in that a holy man only eats what his body can entirely use. The first separate public toilet for men and women appeared at a Paris ball in 1739. For post-elimination administration, the rich have used wool or hemp or linen, while the poor used leaves, and grass or stones or sand or water, and in rural south India, it remains the duty of the right hand to transport food to the mouth, as the left hand is restricted to sanitation ministration.

Many employed a scraper such as a mussel shell or clam shell, until, in 1857, American Joseph Cayetty invented toilet paper, improved upon in 1880 by the British perforated paper company, which sold it in boxes, evolving into a roll in 1907 with the texture of crepe paper. And today, public restrooms offer rolls as large as cheese wheels, from which, studies show, the average tear is 6 sheets and 60% of users examine the paper before flushing.

And all this is preamble to news that the Commerce Subcommittee of the U.S. Congress continues to reject right-thinking efforts to repeal the 1992 Toilet law which outlawed the three-and-a-half gallon flush. Despite testimony by plumbers that multiple flushes are required to wash detritus from low-flow toilets, selfish representatives from freshwater-poor New Mexico and Florida work to defeat the repeal, in the face of testimony that a Porcelain Cartel is smuggling 3.5 gallon toilets across U.S. borders from Canada and Mexico. Americans demand flush-ability and should not be criminalized for rejecting a system which often fails to deal with a cigarette butt, much less the contents, about which, the less said, the better. Restrictions are blessedly absent from our skyscraper public toilets where the pressure is cranked up to reach the 90th floor and a pull on the lever is a whitewater adventure, reminding one of the flow from Hoover Dam on a million gigawatt day; suitable for sandblasting.

Why must the water-deprived inflict universal sufferance? Give the water conservation toilets to New

Mexico. But in Chicago, my hometown, walk three blocks east of downtown and what impedes your forward progress? Sixty miles of H2O. Enough 3 ½ gallon flushes to last till the sun supernovas. Anyway, as to my observation that the concept of an India Toilet Museum is a novelty, Mr. Sinha responded with the question; is it so odd that such a museum exists in a country which daily produces 900 million liters of urine, 237 million gallons, or the equivalent of nearly 279 Olympic-sized swimming pools, or 450 million two-liter bottles of Mountain Dew? And where 135 million kilograms of fecal matter, or 297 million pounds (the equivalent of one and a half times the weight of the U.S. aircraft carrier U.S.S. Nimitz) is excreted daily? Which you'll agree is a shipload.

Ix-Chel, Ma Belle

A woman I know is getting married in Cozumel, and Anita and I can't attend but I composed the following, which I hope is apropos to the occasion.

Long, long ago, in the years before Cozumel had a Roy Rogers Roast Beef and a Hooters, women would travel there to ask the Maya goddess whose name was Ix-Chel to make them pregnant. It was the custom for every Mayan woman on the Yucatan Peninsula, at least once in her lifetime, to row herself across the thirteen miles of sea from Playa Del Carmen, which back then was called Xaman Ha (in the years before it had a T.G.I. Fridays), in a pirogue, which was the word I misspelled in the seventh grade so as not to advance to the National Spelling Bee in Washington, D.C. And they rowed these dugout pirogues---p-i-r-o-g-u-e-s---to Cozumel to lay small baby dolls at the feet of the stone idol of Ix-Chel, the goddess of fertility and concupiscence (which is strong sexual desire), who was the Maya counterpart to the Egyptian goddess Isis. And they brought their tributes to the Ix-Chel ceremonial center which is now a ruins some twenty miles from the main town on the island called San Gervasio, where today, those who have been there will tell you, more than 15 hundred years after its initial construction, the snack bar closes at five.

Now according to Mayan legend, Ix-Chel was a beautiful young woman with long flowing hair and quite large breasts, who fell for Itzamna, the Sun god, and had sex with him, probably because he was so hot. And when her grandfather, who was the Maya version of Thor, found out about the affair, he killed her dead with a bolt of lightning. As she lay dead, grieving dragonflies sang over Ix-Chel for 13 days, at which time she was restored to life and went to live with her lover, Itzamna, in his palace in the sky, where they were wed. And she gave birth to the four Bacabs, who grew up to be the giants, Cauac, Ix, Kan, and Mulac, whose job is holding up the sky at the four cardinal points, north, south, east and west.

But the Sun was very jealous and accused her of sleeping with his brother, who was the morning star. And he kicked her out of heaven, and the Vulture god took her in. Then her husband pursued her to the Vulture god's house and persuaded her to come back with him, and she gave birth to all the other Mayan gods. But he got jealous again and accused her of sleeping around, and every time he would kick her out of heaven he would run after her and beg her to come back and serenade her with a ballad, perhaps something along the lines of; "Ix-Chel, ma belle, sont le mots qui vont tres bien ensemble. Tres bien ensemble." And as time went by, she tired of her husband and his Mr. Big Shot deity attitude, what with his invention of writing and knowledge and calendars and all, and decided to step out on him at night when he wasn't around.

As the moon, she continues to wander the night as she wishes, and departs when the Sun approaches her vicinity in violation of the court order. Her side-kick was The Sky-Serpent, an enormous snake who carried all the water in the heavens in his belly, from which she would fill her enormous jugs with water to pour down on to the Earth in rainstorms, so that rainbows could appear, and Ix-Chel means, "She of rainbows." And when the Earth ends in the year 2012, in a drowning deluge and flood, it will be Ix-Chel who does the pouring.

And she sent her personal favorite birds to decorate her personal favorite island and called the place, Ah-Cuzamil-Peten, or Island of Swallows. She is often depicted in stone glyphs accompanied by companions who fondle her breasts. Because breasts were very important in the worship of Ix-Chel, and a woman visiting Cozumel desirous of fertility, must wade into the water waist-deep and scatter flowers around, and bare her breasts and hold them up and ask Ix-Chel to fill them with milk. Because Ix-Chel was chief in charge of birthing babies and promised to give extra double-dog fertility to any woman who visits her sacred island, which will be the one directly beneath my bride-to-be-friend's personal ovaries as she speaks her wedding vows. Which is a word to the wise by way of a reminder to her that the resort gift shop stocks condoms.

The First Americans: Paleolithic Portugeezers

Back in the year 1590, about the time England invented the madrigal, a Jesuit scholar named Jose de Acosta, who had returned to Spain after fifteen years traveling with the conquistadors in Peru, decided he'd figured out how the Indians of the New World had come to be there. And he wrote a book called the Natural and Moral History of the Indians, in which he set out his theory that the Indians had come from Asia over a land-bridge across the Bering Strait, and, in the 410 years since then, this has been the prevailing logic considered logical by scholars anthropological and archeological.

Until now. Now we are told the Indians came from Spain. A duo of maverick scientists have dropped a heretical bombshell into the backyard of Clovis Man. Clovis Man was named for the New Mexico town northeast of Roswell, near Blackwater Draw, where distinctive spear points were found with the bones of wooly mammoths; stone tips found elsewhere across the Americas. And after the discovery, in 1929, the ancient ancestors of Native Americans were called Clovis Man and modern archeologists have gathered together, here and there, to re-examine the theory of continental settlement, and to share anthropology humor, such as the one where the anthropologist, expressing his amazement over the medicinal constipation-curing properties of a Uruguayan palm plant, exclaims, "With fronds like this, who needs enemas?" And anthropological archeologists Dennis Stanford and Bruce Bradley are causing vexatious botheration among the orthodox with their contention the Indians didn't all come chasing mammoths across the Asian land bridge, but instead paddled over from Spain or Portugal. And the usually snidely-scoffing majority has had its snooty scoffs stifled somewhat by the prominence of the infidels, as Mr. Bradley is a recognized Anasazi expert from Cortez, Colorado, and Mr. Stanford is the Curator of Anthropology at the Smithsonian Institution.

And they figure it this way. Way back in the Paleolithic, somewhere on the Iberian Peninsula which bulges from the south of France to the Rock of Gibraltar, lived the Solutreans; hunter-gatherers who fished from skin boats like the Eskimos use, and who, this new school of thought informs us, sailed the ocean blue seventeen thousand years prior to 1492. And at this historical epoch, by which time islanders of the South Pacific had already been sailing the open sea for twenty thousand years, these truly ancient mariners likely followed the coastline of Europe north and took a left from Scandinavia to Iceland and Greenland before following the eastern coast of North America south to the wooded shores from New England to Florida. The Clovis camp envisions its Mongol-skulled hunters skipping down the prehistorical Trans-Alaskan highway into the southwest around 11,500 BC. But Stanford and Bradley point to artifacts from sites in Pennsylvania, Virginia, and South Carolina which date from 12,500 to 16,000 BC, one to four thousand years earlier than the

ETA of Clovis, and say the stone spear tips are indistinguishable from the spear tips of the Solutreans.

A new believer, Kent State archeologist Kenneth Tankersley, is quoted thusly: "There is no question about it...there are only two places in the world and two times this tool technology appears---Solutrea and Clovis." So now we are to believe that the tribes whose domain spread from Fort Duquesne to Fort Wayne and across the Great Plain to the Rocky Mountain chain, whooping 'round the wagon train, and shot at by John Wayne, and written about by the Gray who was Zane, were, in the main, from Spain. And there is irony in the possibility that, when Iberian explorers claimed the New World for Spain, the indigenous population had, eons ago, already been there and done that.

Of course barring DNA comparison, the question of whether Native Americans are direct descendants of ancient Portugeezers is academic and debatable, like whether Norwegian Leif Erikson predated Columbus in North America by 500 years, which recalls to mind the one about how when Leif Erikson sailed home he found his name missing from the town roll to which the head population counter apologized, saying, "I must have taken Leif off my census."

Chapter 5—Food and Beverage

What's the Proper Age for a Fake I.D.?

My boy Jonathan recently turned 20, which got me to thinking about drinking, and about what age is an appropriate age to take a drink. When I was 18 it was legal to drink 3.2 beer in Ohio, which we came to quickly learn would provide just as much alcohol as high powered beer were one to drink twice as many, which we always made sure to do. And those were in the unenlightened years when we youth could still take pride in having gotten blitzed, which was a diminutive of blitzkrieg, rather than a derivative of Blatz, but it was certainly possible to experience a Blatz blitz, in addition to a blitz induced by Schlitz.

But our legislators subsequently changed the statutes, likely as a result of my generation having put the top down on our Triumph Spitfires and driven down the sidewalk at 3 AM one too many times.

I harbor no illusions my son is a stranger to the brewmaster's elixir, in that on a family vacation a couple of years ago, the drinking age in Mexico was 18, and with his all-inclusive wrist band it is doubtless he made the acquaintance of cerveza fria, because it is the nature of teenagers to wish greatly for that which is prohibited to them. And we whose fake IDs were dog-eared by 18 feel a trifle hypocritical wrestling with the issue of criminalizing kids old enough to pour into the draft but too young to pour a draft.

And when contemplating issues ethical and moral, I find it comforting to invoke the letters, WWJD, and commence to wondering, What Would Jesus Drink? Beer has been consumed by man since the dawn of misty prehistory in that it fairly makes itself. Water mixed with barley, or the water drained from sodden grains, left unattended, upon which stray yeast cells would settle from the air, turns to beer, and having discovered this, early nomads stopped nomadding and settled down to the serious business of agriculture for purposes of propagating this miraculous gift of nature; the accidental byproduct of this being civilization. Beer was drunk by the Babylonians, and the oldest recipe unearthed is on a cuneiform tablet bearing a 4 thousand year old Sumerian formula. Beer was, by archeological evidence, brewed in ancient Egypt. The Assyrians drank it. England's King Henry the Second invoked a Saladin Tithe, which was a tax on beer to pay for the Crusades, in which some searched for the Holy Grail, which was Our Master's mug. Beer figured in where the Pilgrims decided to drop anchor. A Mayflower passenger's journal reads thusly on the decision to land at Plymouth, quoting: "...we could not now take time for further search or consideration, our victuals being much spent, especially our beer."

It has been said by a variety of individuals who own accordions, that, "In Heaven There Is No Beer." But it can be demonstrated that Christ himself said there is no Prohibition in Paradise. At the last supper, after instructing the others to raise their glasses of wine, and "Drink ye all of it," he said the following (Matthew 26, verse 29): "I will not drink of this fruit of the vine until that day when I drink it new with you in My Father's Kingdom," assuring those who believe in him that there will be an afterlife of the party, and it is not surprising that the Lord was a drinking man because he was a traditional Jew and took wine as was the custom from an early age.

In the Bible, alcoholic beverages are divided into two categories: Strong drink and wine. Scholars take strong drink to mean a fermented grain beverage and wine to be a fermented fruit beverage, and so 'strong drink,' would be Biblical beer. In the Old Testament, Proverbs 31, verses 6&7 instruct: "Give strong drink unto him that is ready to perish, and wine unto those that be of heavy heart. Let him drink, and forget his poverty and remember his misery no more." It was the Apostle Paul who wrote to young pastor Timothy, 1st Timothy, chapter 5, verse 23: "No longer drink water exclusively, but use a little wine for the sake of your stomach." Of course it was Jesus who turned water into wine at the wedding in Cana and kept it coming from the bottomless jug, in that he knew by heart as a rabbi Psalm 104 which begins, "Bless the Lord, O my soul," praising God for creating, quote, "Wine, which makes man's heart glad."

There are two schools of thought with regard to drinking at any age. Robert Benchley said, "Drinking makes such fools of people, and people are such fools to begin with, that it is compounding a felony." Although it was Hunter S. Thompson who said, "I hate to advocate alcohol, drugs, violence, and insanity to anyone, but they've always worked for me."

I have a confession to make and it is that I permitted my boy to drink at an early age. When Jonathan was 14, I sent him to Greece with a youth tour group hosted by a cousin of mine who is a scholar of Greek history, who warned me that upon occasion an innkeeper might offer his group a round of some local Greek wine or liqueur, as is the custom. And so I gave permission for Jonathan to participate in toasts if toasts there be. And so when he returned I was not surprised that Jonathan told the story of how he lifted a glass in convivial fraternity with fellow travelers at some bistro in a Greek coastal village and I asked after the identity of the special local beverage peculiar to that rustic region which was provided to him by the locals of that locale, to which he replied, "Southern Comfort." Which, you'll agree, is anecdotally unsatisfying.

The Murder of Claudius is Solved; No Arrest Imminent

On the 13th of October in the year 54 Anno Domini, Emperor Claudius, supreme exalted executive and commander-in-chief of the Roman Empire, sat down for his favorite dish, a bowl of bright orange mushrooms which were the rage in Rome. Some 12 hours later, the 64-year-old Claudius was dead, his departure setting the stage for the elevation of Nero, Rome's psychotic fiddler, to assume the throne. From day one, murder was suspected. And authorities in Baltimore have announced they have solved the crime and named a suspect and revealed the murder weapon.

Dr. William Valente, a professor at the University of Maryland School of Medicine, says it was muscarine poisoning. Muscarine is a toxic alkaloid found in the Amanita Muscaria, also known as Fly-Agaric, a bright red large fungus that sprouts from trees and whose fully-extended parasol can measure ten inches. Many believe this mushroom is the plant called Soma of ancient Hindu legend, the pressed juices from which caused an ecstatic altered state of consciousness and hallucinations. In the early 1700s, academic Filip Johann Von Strahlenberg studied the use of the Amanita Muscaria as an intoxicant among Siberian tribesmen. The wealthy would pour boiling water over the mushrooms to make a liquor, which they would drink and become euphoric. The poor tribesmen would wait outside the domiciles of the party-goers, who would, as the spirit moved them, come outside and urinate into their wooden bowls, from which the poor would drink unto intoxication, the psychoactive properties of the mushroom having passed, unaltered, through the human body. Wrote sociologist Waldemar Jochelson of this same Siberian custom in the early 20th century, "The person intoxicated with the Fly-Agaric sits quietly rocking from side to side, even taking part in conversations. Suddenly his eyes dilate, he begins to gesticulate convulsively, conversing with people he imagines he sees, and sings and dances. To continue the intoxication additional doses are necessary and the drunkard will consume his own urine to prolong the hallucinations"—close quote.

Anyhow, Baltimore's Dr. Valente says Claudius's wife Agrippina wished her son by another man, Nero, to succeed Claudius, while Claudius' own son was still a minor and unable to assume power. And so Dr. Valente confirms centuries-old suspicions alleging that Agrippina mixed in toxic mushrooms among the benign, which her gluttonous spouse shoveled into his capacious abdomen. According to contemporary accounts, after his mushroom dinner, Claudius developed red-eye, a runny nose and a drool, stomach cramps and diarrhea. The description of muscarine poisoning in today's medical texts reads: Symptoms include excessive salivation, sweating, tears, severe vomiting and diarrhea, visual disturbances, irregular pulse, decreased blood pressure, and difficulty breathing. Respiratory failure may result from large doses. So it was Agrippina in the palace with a mushroom. And it would appear that she got away with it.

But it is axiomatic that what goes around, comes around, and her boy Nero decided to have his mom murdered, and thought about poison, but decided on drowning, and bade her bon voyage on a cruise boat designed to sink, and when she survived and swam to shore, he had her stabbed to death.

These plotting machinations recall to mind the story of Emperor Augustus' daughter Julia, an aunt of Claudius, who was married to Agrippa, Augustus' choice to succeed him as emperor. And when Agrippa died unexpectedly, Julia married Tiberius, who was Augustus' next choice to succeed him. And Julia was a nymphomaniac who slept with a Roman legion of noblemen and equestrians and was never faithful to any of her three husbands and her father became at last exasperated with her jumping into bed with every Marcus, Lucius, and Crassus, and banished her to a lonely island. And the Roman writer Macrobius, who collected the jokes of notable Romans, recounted Julia's response to someone aware of her promiscuity, who remarked, marveling, that, despite her many lovers, all of her children looked like her husband, Agrippa; to which Julia retorted, "Numquam enim nisi navi plena tollo vectorem," which means, "I never take a passenger on board until the cargo hold is full."

George R. Notel, II

It was while doing an Internet search on beer in ancient Mesopotamia for another story altogether, that I encountered George R. Notel, Jr. George works in computer support for the School of Public Policy at Georgia Tech University. And when he was still going to Georgia Tech---well, let him tell you in his own words, posted on his home page; "I turned 21 on April 2, 1995, and since then, I have not had the same beer twice. I drank almost never before turning 21, so I am new to beer drinking. I only drink two beers a night, and only on weekends. Here, I am providing a list of beers I have had, as well as my opinions." And so George commenced to log a journal---a diary---of his encounters with a variety of beers, his intent to love 'em and leave 'em, never returning to the same bottle twice. And, for several years, he has kept to his personal goal of tasting the beers of the world without ever becoming pixilated. His rule: a maximum of two beers per night; only on weekends. From time to time, he would issue a bulletin, such as in the fall of 1997, when he informed visitors to his web site that he had spent five months in some location not conducive to drinking beer, and that, during that period, he had taken no beer and he was announcing the resumption of his beer consumption at that time.

Some typical entries: Weihenstephan Original—quoting, "I spent three dollars on this beer, so I was pretty sure I was going to finish it. It was okay." Red Ridge Ale---"The beer bottle was red. I tried it and enjoyed it. I was not too surprised that I did like it, as I am a fan of red beers." Samuel Adams Cranberry Lambic---"Finally, a Sam Adams beer I like! I am not a fan of cranberry sauce, but I tried it." There are other entries such as "Four beers in a row that I liked. Hopefully the streak will continue." And of Bad Frog Beer he writes, "This one I bought because of the name. The frog on the front is giving the finger. Granted, he only has four fingers, so it could be argued it's not his middle, but I think that's what the brewers wanted." And the chronicles ended abruptly with the announcement in August of 1999 that he had gotten married and as a result had less time to squander on his beer project.

And so I E-mailed George to discover whether he has suspended his beer-tasting forever, and he replied that with one child born and another on the way he hasn't the time, but does allow as how he intends to drink another beer just as soon as he finds a local package store which sells them as single bottles, as he has no intention of ever consuming six of a kind. Since he turned 21 in 1995, he has never wavered from spurning the intoxicating siren's song of Bacchus—never having gotten waffled in his entire life-experience of beer drinking.

And I hope his marriage succeeds, because the evidence points to George being a man who can't maintain a relationship. One cannot know a beer in a single encounter; a one night stand. George must lower the barriers he has constructed around him and let the beer in. To embrace it and quaff heartily from the flagon of experience and eat the yeasty bread of life like a man rather than scurrying out the mouse hole to snack on an occasional crumb. You can't claim to have had a real relationship with a wheaty dark-amber porter until you have informed the bartender at two in the morning in a weepy slur that if only Becky Lydon hadn't become a Nixon volunteer during the McGovern campaign you would have stayed together and been happy.

I offer the advice of those wiser than myself and recommend, in the words of the chorus in *Threepenny Opera,* "Drink, drink, for wine inspires us, and fires us with courage, love and joy." Aristophanes said more than four centuries before the Son of God himself turned water into wine, "When men drink, then they are rich and successful and win lawsuits and are happy and help their friends. Quickly, bring me a beaker, so that I may wet my mind and say something clever." English poet Alfred Housman called beer indispensable to the human spirit when he wrote, "The troubles of our proud and angry dust, are from eternity, and shall not fail. Bear them we can, and if we can, we must. Shoulder the sky, my lad, and drink your ale." F. Scott Fitzgerald said "While you live, drink!—for once dead, you never shall return." It was Victor Hugo who wrote in *Les Miserables,* "Upon the first goblet he read this inscription, monkey wine; upon the second, lion wine; upon the third, sheep wine: upon the fourth, swine wine. These four inscriptions the four descending degrees of drunkenness; the first, that which enlivens; the second, that which irritates; the third, that which stupefies; and last, that which brutalizes." So with Victor Hugo I lift a glass to wish that all your goblets are filled with monkey wine. And didn't Jesus buy a round in the Upper Room and command, "Drink ye all of it?" Attend to the word of the Lord.

The Potato Shamus

You will likely not disagree with the statement that scientists are doing all manner of things that we will see and say "I wish you hadn't done that," and I am not only talking about altering fruit flies to grow eyes on their legs. Those among us whose favorite moments in science class were when audio-visual would reel up *Hemo the Magnificent* with Dr. Frank Baxter are often discomfited by the slide-rule Sammies who dare to push their technological Roto-tillers into the Almighty's organic humus.

But where science is making positive inroads, as I see it, is in the field of forensics, and I direct your attention to a story little known outside professional potato detective circles. Unbeknownst to us civilians who are scrupulous about using our potatoes in a lawful manner, the Idaho Potato Commission is vigilant about monitoring interstate potato shipments for criminal activity. And it happens that an informer, identified only as a retired Wisconsin potato grower, some five years ago, was patrolling the produce aisles at a major grocery chain, and this keen-eyed potato investigator spotted some round white spuds labeled Idaho, a provenance which his experience caused him to fiercely doubt. And so this informer dropped a dime on the Idaho Potato Commission, which apparently employs investigative potato agents, wearing badges and fedoras.

And I imagine their reports back to Boise read something along the lines of; "Her head nestled against my shoulder holster and she moved my hand up her body until I could feel there was no marvel of engineering connected to her bra because there was no bra…and the studded belt she wore was the key to the whole ensemble, and when it unsnapped the whole affair came apart in a whisper of black satin that folded back against the trash compactor until all of her reflected the exhaust fan light from above the avocado stove, and there was no sound but that of our breathing and the potatoes boiling."

So they called in these potato shamuses and sent the potatoes to the Idaho Potato crime lab, which subjected the suspect potatoes to Mineral Element Profile Analysis, and ascertained that there was no way these potatoes were native to Idaho. It turns out that as potatoes grow beneath the Earth, they take up trace elements of their native potato patch, and trace elements of Wisconsin dirt are as different from trace elements of Idaho dirt as your fingerprint from mine. And if this were Dragnet, a Jack Webb production, the announcer would say,"In a moment, the results of that trial." And after the commercial, but before the sweaty hand hammered the stamp of Mark VII Productions into steel to the sound of tympani and anvil, the announcer would return to intone; "Potato Specialties, Inc, of Blue Island, Illinois, was found to have perpetrated potato fraud, and its principals have admitted to packing three million, four hundred thousand pounds of Wisconsin potatoes in potato sacks marked Grown in Idaho, and have each agreed to pay the Idaho Potato Commission one hundred thousand dollars for this felonious potato peccadillo perpetration." And I have said it before and I'll say it again, Idaho is the name of a state, not a potato, and Wisconsin's are Russets too. Or Norkotahs. But we should not abide charlatans in any guise, and it is reassuring that the potato eyes of Idaho are upon interstate vegetable commerce.

I visited the Commission's Internet site to obtain contact numbers, and additionally learned that the average American eats 142.7 pounds of potatoes each year, 59 pounds frozen, 48 pounds fresh, 18 pounds dehydrated, 2 pounds canned, and 16 pounds as potato chips, and that two "Grown in Idaho" seals and 8.75 can obtain a 16 inch Idaho Potato Buddy Doll, a good deal for parents who imagine encouraging children to play with a plush toy of a Russet Burbank potato with legs is not disturbing.

Anyhow, Mel Anderson, who is the plenipotentiary potato potentate presiding over the monolithic Idaho

Potato Commission, says the two hundred thousand dollars extracted by this lawsuit will be used to buy air time for running TV commercials for the purpose of restoring the reputation of Idaho potatoes. And at headquarters, I was put in touch with noted potato attorney Patrick Kole, the top legal mind at the Idaho Potato Commission, and asked him why this case took four years to settle, to which he wryly observed, quoting, "In this country, the wheels of justice turn slowly," unquote. Or he may have said, "grind slowly;" I wasn't really paying all that much attention.

The Fruit Painter

On one of those TV appraisal shows, a woman brought a small painting of some fruit and I was surprised when the appraiser expected she could get twenty-eight hundred dollars for it and was intrigued when he revealed the creator of it to be an artist named Carducius Plantagenet Ream, who turns out to be the best dad-burned American fruit painter of the 19th century.

And I have long been drawn to fruit paintings, as they require no expertise in art history or theology or ethnography for interpretation; as one can clearly see that this is fruit, and doesn't it look good, and don't I wish I had a nice Bartlett pear right about now? And on the walls of the world's art galleries resides evidence of the existence of a vast trade, over centuries, in fruit pictures which were apparently desired for purposes of hanging them on the wall and contemplating them and wondering when in the world somebody would get around to inventing television. And to fulfill the voracious insatiable demand by the general public for fruit pictures, a cadre of young 19th century American painters set about filling canvas with casabas and currants and guavas and grapefruit and honeydews and huckleberries. And foremost among them was Carducius Plantagenet Ream.

Why Mr. & Mrs. Ream, of Lancaster, Ohio, named their first born child Carducius (perhaps from the Latin Carduus; meaning thistle) and Plantagenet (The surname of the 14 kings of England from 1154 to 1485, descended from the daughter of Henry the First and Count Geoffrey, who was called Plantagenet because he wore a sprig of bramble-bush [genista in Latin] in his hat), is lost to history, but it can be theorized his signature is generally rendered C.P. Ream to conserve paint. And I visited a web site called AskArt.com, which lists art transactions from coast to coast, and found that over a recent interval, fruit paintings by Carducius Plantagenet Ream have come up at auction eight times, and have fetched premium prices. A 16 x 20 inch picture of some handsome cantaloupes sold for seven thousand dollars in New York. A smaller painting of a single slice of watermelon went for 33 hundred dollars at Christies in Los Angeles. An oil depiction of a peach, an orange, and grapes of several varieties on a linen tablecloth beside a vase of flowers, sold for 9 thousand in Milford, Connecticut. And a painting of a two large grapefruits, an apple, a pear, and a plum on a tabletop, beside evidence of a marriage proposal having been made and accepted (notes and a corsage), sold for 27,600 dollars, which, at 15 inches by 19 inches, is 90 dollars per square inch. There is money in the fruit picture trade. And it turns out that a young Carducius Plantagenet Ream learned to paint Ohio fruit and went on to paint the fruit of New York City and Cincinnati, prior to taking up residence in Chicago in 1878 to become the city's pre-eminent fruit painter. His painting entitled "Just Gathered," was the first painting by an actual Chicago painter to be acquired by the Art Institute. And so I visited the Art Institute to admire a 106 year-old plethora of plums preserved by C.P. in 1895, and a fine bunch of plums it is.

So prosperous and popular was he that his fruit pictures were reproduced as prints by Louis Prang and Company of Boston and advertised in catalogues as dining room pictures, providing income affording him the luxury of travel to the continent to paint the fruit of England and Germany. And Carducius Plantagenet Ream had a younger brother named Morston Constantine Ream, to whom he recommended the rewarding and glamorous lifestyle of a fruit painter, and who came to specialize in fruits and desserts, or what one writer called, "opulent still-life comestibles."

And while dawdling on AskArt.com, I began a specialized collection of my own, of what I consider to be remarkable examples of painter names, as, in addition to Carducius Plantagenet Ream, I encountered fine oils by Squeak Carnwath, Wickenworth Gay, Dawson Watson Dawson, Letta Crapo Smith, Oscar Florianus Bluemner, Ignaz Marcel Gaugengigl, and Otto Botto.

Jesus Never Ate a Potato and Other Facts

Geraldine Benz, from the sylvan glades of suburban Oswego, sent me a book of poems about potatoes and one of them goes, "Tonight, in Mexico, I gouge eyes from small, round, red potatoes, throw them in a pot of water. When the water begins to boil, Mr. Potato Head, abandoned, forgotten for years, bobs to the top of the pot, stares with loud, accusing eyes into mine. Silencio! I cry—por favor, silencio!—and slam the lid down."

Which came to mind as I read where the American Dietetic Association declares that millions of years of evolution on this planet created carbon-based life forms perfectly suited for the dietary processing of foods containing neutral compounds of carbon, hydrogen and oxygen, as they are found in sugars, starches, and cellulose---or, in other words; carbohydrates. The American Dietetic Association would like to add that most of the people in the world live on grains and potatoes, and that without carbohydrates the survival of animal life on the planet would be doubtful.

Which is just the American Dietetic Association's way of calling Dr. Robert Atkins and his carnivores bone-brained beef-wits. The growing cult of Atkins shuns carbohydrates and sugars and adheres to a protein menu of unlimited meat, cheese and eggs with no sweets, rice, pasta, potatoes, or bread, despite the Lord's Prayer plea to be given our daily bread. And Jesus called himself bread and spoke often of bread because, from what we read in the New Testament the Son of God and contemporaries ate a high carbohydrate diet, what with the beans and lentils and barley and toasted grains, in that fish and lamb were consumed on rare occasions.

And one wonders what fine food-related Bible quotations we missed because Jesus never ate a potato. Never had a one of 'em. Not once in the whole Bible does the word appear, which is because the place where the almighty everlasting omnipotent Jehovah planted it, in the eleventh verse of the book of Genesis, where it is written that God declared "Let the earth sprout vegetation, plants yielding seed after their kind…and it was so," was high in the Andes near Lake Titicaca, which is the Inca word for "lake of the snickering fourth grade schoolboys."

More valuable than all the gold looted from the indigenous New World treasuries by the conquistadors, the descendants of Andean potatoes today constitute the fourth most important food crop in the world after wheat, rice, and corn. And Jonathan Swift wrote that "Bread is the staff of life" and Pilgrim Plymouth Colony founder Edward Winslow wrote that "Corn is the staff of life."

And in that there exists this divergence of opinion might I suggest that it is the potato which is the staff of life, in that there are six billion people alive, and more than one in six consume nature's perfect super-food as a significant part of their diet, including in Israel where a second-coming Jesus would today find potatoes growing beside the sea of Galilee, because, where water is scarce, potatoes provide a maximum by-weight yield per expenditure of water compared with other crops. And, like the miracle of the loaves, from a single potato can many be created, cut up; the eyes planted.

The average potato contains 120 calories, is low in sodium, high in potassium and is a major source of complex carbohydrates and vitamin B-6 and more than one fourth of the recommended daily vitamin C fried, boiled or baked; an even higher amount microwaved. Its absence from the Bible once caused inhabitants of Scotland to refuse to eat it, but the Scots later became so dependent upon the tuber that an old Scotch lament goes, "What good is he to me? For three days he has not even brought me a potato." And it is written in haiku; "Imperfect sphere—curls into self—must rot to resurrect." Speaking of resurrection, one doesn't have to be without sin to divide a few potatoes among the many. Just boil and mash.

But back to the Andes—I receive Archaeology magazine and it just frosts my cinnamon buns that the scholars have taken to spelling Inca with a K. There is no earthly reason to spell it with a K since it has been pronounced the same way with a C for hundreds of years and they've just taken to doing it out of high-hatted arrogance, as the archaeological academicians, who spell archeology with an ae, mount their contemptuous condescending cornstarchy-collared snooty-sniffy phonemic high-horses. Join me in protest, will you? The E-mail address at Archaeology is letters@archaeology.org. Let's all convey the message: "Inca with a C is good enough for me."

Everything I Know is Wrong

I know little enough without learning that everything I think I know is wrong, which occurred to me when I read the story about scientific research which shows that women at high risk of getting breast cancer can protect against it by smoking cigarettes, and another scientific study that shows eating red meat can prevent diabetes.

Purdue scientists discovered that a type of fat called CLA, which resides in red meat and cheese, prevents adult-onset diabetes in rats. And scientists at Women's College Hospital in Toronto found that women who have high-risk breast cancer genes have half the risk of actually developing breast cancer if they smoke cigarettes, which apparently burns off estrogen which otherwise would stimulate breast tissue. And of course after they proclaimed how good red meat and smoking are for certain people, the scientists were quick to add that the contraindications of smoking far outweigh the benefits, so what exactly was the purpose of the press conference aside from providing a pretext for a continental breakfast?

Anyway, much of what I learned in college has, for the most part, leaked out of memory, probably because when I read in the brochure that Ohio University was a fountain of knowledge, I went there to drink. It is troubling that much of what little I know may be incorrect, such as my childhood belief that a Jehovah's Witness Assembly Hall was where they manufactured them. It was Nobel Prize-winning physicist Richard Feynman who said shortly before he died, "I was born not knowing and have only had a little time to change that here and there."

There are many questions whose answers remain beyond my grasp. Like how they figure the pay for the trumpet players at the symphony. I went to the Chicago

Symphony with my wife, and I couldn't believe it when Anita told me the tickets were 91 dollars each, because that was the most we ever paid to go to the symphony, and during Brahms Piano Concerto No.2 in B-flat Major, Opus 83, I counted the number of musicians on the stage and there were seventy-seven, including the guest conductor. So, if they split my 91 dollars, each of them would make $1.18. Which seems a bit miserly because I tip the pizza deliveryman more than that. But the strings did most of the work, and the two trumpet players sitting in the back might as well have bought a ticket themselves for all they did. A definition of sloth could include the phrase, "as indolent as a trumpet player at a Brahms Piano Concerto." They didn't even hold their trumpets as if they were preparing to play. They put them down on the floor and picked them up and tooted them for maybe 8 bars at the climax and put them down again. And that's a 48-minute piece. If I were a violin player I'd be resentful of the trumpets. They are like the bridge tenders who get paid all the same whether a boat comes along or not. On the other hand, in the second half just about everybody was putting in sweat equity on the Shostakovich.

    And here is another unsolved mystery to me. I was doing some tiling work at my house and I think I did a really good job. And the guy at the Tile Barn gave me a bottle of silicon sealant to protect the grout from moisture and I read the directions and it says wait 28 days before applying. Why 28 days? What is going to happen in 28 days? And how will the tile know when 28 days are up? And if I apply the sealant before 28 days, what is anybody going to do about it? Following much contemplation, I concluded this is an inside practical joke among tile masons and tile setters and tile finishers who will elbow one another in the ribs and whisper mockingly of amateurs like myself, "he waited the 28 days", and chortle till they snort. I have half a mind to throw caution to the wind and seal the tile tonight and the consequences be damned.

And on the one hand, it troubles me, that, about most things, I don't know chalk from cheese. But on the other hand the good news is that it will never be said of me, "They killed him because he knew too much."

My Dinner at Charlie Trotter's (Now defunct. RIP Charlie)

On my wedding anniversary I chose to go for the triple points so I'll have some points banked, which I can draw upon when I inevitably run a deficit, and so I took Anita to Charlie Trotter's. And I'd never been there before, but it is well known that, to the food critics, he's like Obi-Wan Kohlrabi. And the restaurant was a nondescript brick row house, and even the inside wasn't fancy, and gives one no outward clue that, with the amount one is about to pay for dinner, one could buy two tickets to Tampa on Southwest Airlines with a fourteen-day advance purchase.

And the food was so fancy I had to write down what we had, which was not easy because, unlike many of the restaurants I frequent, Charlie Trotter's discourages one from writing on the place mats. When you open the menu, you discover your choices are two. You choose either the all-meat, or the all-vegetable courses, and the vegetable course costs seventy dollars and the meat course costs ninety dollars. And although the vegetable menu lists appealing culinary experiments such as Ragu of Early Spring Morels, Fava Beans, Haricot Verts and Baby Leeks in their own juices, and Raddicchio and Yellowfoot Mushroom Risotto with Stuffed Turnip and Red Wine Emulsion, we both went with meat, so I'm a hundred and eighty dollars lighter right out of the starting gate and that's without wine.

Which is a whole other story; because the wine list arrives in a leather-bound portfolio like the kind one might see at the national archives containing the Japanese Surrender or the Louisiana Purchase. And on the one hand, you have your St. Julien Chateau Leoville Las Cases 1959, for about the price of a really good home entertainment center with fifty-inch screen and surround sound. Or there's the Schloss Reicharts-Hausen Leibenshalter Sprechling Halbtrocken Reisling Alsace Lower Valley 1941, which sounds like something with which the Fuhrer would have toasted the annexation of the Sudetenland. At the high end, they will bring you a bottle of Pomeral Cheateau Latour-a-Pomerol 1961, for five thousand dollars. Just for the one. For five thousand dollars I would expect to be sipping it in a Super Bowl skybox, poured by Joey Heatherton in go-go boots. So I ordered the 1995 Duckhorn Souvignon Blanc from the Napa Valley for twenty-two dollars for a half-bottle; which at Charlie Trotter's translates, in wine terms, to generic.

And then they bring the food, and it comes in seven courses with seven different men in nice suits escorting each plate to formally introduce you to your entrée. And after the Steamed Catfish with Lobster Sauce, followed by the Smoked Atlantic Salmon, Maine Lobster and Caviar with Jicama, Blended Horseradish and Spicy Herb Sauce; and after the Casco Bay Codfish and Diver Scallop with Braised Cardoon and Curry Emulsion; and after the California Pigeon Breast with Crispy Polenta, Braised Red Cabbage, Tiny Shitakes and Cumin-Infused Broth; and after the Iowa Lamb Loin with Caramelized Rutabaga, Braised Legumes and Meat Juices, you'd think you wouldn't have room for dessert. But you would be wrong, because all these entrees come on really big plates with brightly hued sauces drizzled around like a Jackson Pollock painting, but the portions are microscopic---like a prop from *Honey, I Shrunk the Dinner*. And when they say, "comes with corn" they mean, like, two kernels, and I know they don't grow real big, but if one is going to serve pigeon breasts, I feel that serving any fewer than eight violates the Geneva Convention. I only got one.

Then they bring out the desserts, which are really very good, and they bring each diner six different kinds, all of which are the size of a Milk Dud. But for all you guys who are looking for a nice place to take a girl, I'd have to say, despite the pricey menu, it is worth it, because, although it isn't written right on the menu, it goes without saying that after an evening at Charlie Trotter's, one is guaranteed that sex will break out within the hour.

In Defense of Pizza

Sometimes it is not only right but necessary to kill the messenger, and never so necessary as when the message is that we should eat less pizza. Nutritionists at the Center for Science in the Public Interest, America's foremost issuer of news bulletins best kept to themselves, convened a gathering of the media to proclaim that more cheese on one's pizza means more crust in one's arteries, and recommended meatless veggie pizzas for everybody. It turns out that two slices of Pizza Hut's Stuffed Crust Pepperoni Lover's pizza deliver more than eight hundred calories and a day's worth of saturated fat and sodium. Chief buzz-kill nutritionist Jayne Hurley is quoted as saying, "You need cheese stuffed into a pizza crust like you need reverse liposuction to force more fat under your skin," as well as mocking Domino's Cheesy Bread as an odd accompaniment to an entrée which is mainly cheese and bread. "Please!" ejaculates Ms. Hurley, in a voice dripping with sniffy condescension. Defending right-thinking Americans who spend thirty billion dollars per annum on pizza, Pizza Hut boss Mike Rawlings suggests, in his words, "I think people are a little tired of being told what not to eat," close quote.

And these cheesy Chicken-Littles are the same people who once declared that Bennigans and Chili's and TGI Fridays and Planet Hollywood and the Hard Rock Café and Houlihan's serve entrées with a fat content equivalent to sucking through a straw right out of the Hellman's jar. And they are the same people who told us Taco Bell Taco Salad is nothing more than assisted suicide. These are the people who tipped us that we should get discount coupons for angioplasty with every industrial-sized tub of movie popcorn. These are the people who believe the waiter who brings the plate of fettuccine Alfredo should be charged with attempted manslaughter. The people who say eating Chinese is the same as lining up at a salt lick. And I believe I speak for us all when I say someone should shut these people up by shoving a stick of butter down their throats.

But there is a consistent silver-lining string, which runs through all these studies by fast-food alarmists who will not rest until our nation sits down to a Thanksgiving dinner of soy-curd and rice-cakes. There is a single common denominator in all these pronouncements that eventually switches on the light bulb over one's head. The most recent study declares that a single slice of Pizza Hut's Big New Yorker Sausage pizza "does more damage than a Big Mac," and warns, "While most people wouldn't eat a second Big Mac, many people reach for a third or fourth slice of pizza." A previous caveat indicted an Applebee's mushroom cheeseburger for containing fat equivalent to a Big Mac plus a banana split plus a couple of doughnuts. Another study alleges that eating a Denny's Grand Slam is like eating six Big Macs. And that a jumbo tub of movie popcorn contains more fat than eight Big Macs. And that fettuccine Alfredo is as fatty as twelve Big Macs. So we can conclude from this that the moral of the story---the lesson to be learned---the conclusion to be drawn---the general proposition to be gleaned---the universal truth to be postulated from this is that we should all just eat at McDonalds. In all of these studies, it turns out that a single Big Mac is better than anything. Nobody is going to eat twelve Big Macs; so one Big Mac is nature's perfect super-food. In fact, once the insurance industry is apprised of these statistics, one might expect that eating regularly at McDonald's might qualify one for a lower rate.

Cod Almighty

I have been reading an interesting book about the history of codfish. It is entitled Cod. And cod played a key role in the history of western civilization, as Europeans discovered that cod, filleted and air-dried in the sun covered in salt…would harden and be preserved and would keep for a very long time; and even when as dry and stiff and hard as a canoe paddle, they could beat it with hammers and boil it to soften, and eat it, and it was preserved cod that made possible the long ocean voyages of discovery.

And it turns out that with the no-meat-on-Friday and the forty-days-of-Lent edict, the Catholic Church made the fortunes of cod fishermen, and with each Friday cod merchants got richer because salt-cod was the best tasting and longest-lasting dried fish; much in demand among the majority of Catholics who couldn't afford fresh fish. And the Basques had more to sell than anybody, and the Scandinavians saw no Basques at their fishing grounds, nor did the British or the French, and the Basques kept their source secret and when Jacques Cartier discovered the mouth of the St. Lawrence Seaway and claimed the region for France, his log notes the presence, nearby, of one thousand Basque fishing boats. The Basques had presumably been fishing in North America for years before Columbus arrived but thought it good business to keep quiet about it.

And it was cod that made New England prosperous and built the city of Boston and it was said you could walk on the backs of the fish off Cape Cod, by the old salts who would pull in their nets heavy with ten-pound cod as they sang, "Glo'ster girls they have no combs, Heave Heave Away! They comb their hair with codfish bones, Heave Away, Fair Mary." And I've said it before but "All Sea Shanties, All the Time" is a format begging for airing to an underserved demographic.

Anyway, it occurred to me that I could not tell the dried-cod story without having eaten it myself, and so I went to the fish market and I bought a two-pound slab of dried salt-cod. And you have to soak it to remove the salt and so I put it in a bucket in my garage, which was likely the only one in my neighborhood containing a soaking 2 ½ foot-long dried Norwegian salt-cod.

I was going to soak it in the house, but was disabused of that idea by my wife, whose open-mouthed silence upon my arrival home, I at first mistook for stunned appreciation of my cod-piece and its prodigious size, but who then found words to inquire first as to whether I had lost my mind. And Anita reminded me of the imminent arrival of houseguests, and promised me that, if my science project left a lingering odor of boiled cod in the house, my life would be made a living hell for all eternity.

So, from the book, I took a recipe for codfish chowder from early New Hampshire congressman Daniel Webster, whose chowder is considered standard for that period. And cod meat has virtually no fat and is more than 18% protein, and when cod is dried and the portion of flesh that is water has evaporated, its protein becomes concentrated to nearly 80%. Today's restaurants prepare cod as a delicate flavored whitefish, less fishy than most. But the early Americans wanted no part of delicate, requiring more flavor, which meant more salt. Webster's recipe called for the rendering of salt pork, also called fatback, which I found in the meat area of the grocery in which also reside portions of a pig's facial features. I fried the salty fatback till the fat was melted and tossed in onions till golden and water and potatoes and chunks of my salt-cod and a chopped tomato and some cayenne pepper and then scalded-milk and heavy cream, and sat down to a steaming bowlful of hypertension and atherosclerosis, and can report that it was very flavorful if you were accustomed to dining at a salt lick. And afterwards, I returned to the store for the Glade plug-ins but discovered that they now have a spray they call the Neutralizer with just the right amount of plant and herb extracts to leave a clean, natural freshness rather than a heavy, floral fragrance, but, as of the last time I spoke with Anita, the jury was still out. Of course, now that the North Atlantic Cod fisheries are closed, in an attempt to restore the codfish population, restaurants have substituted other whitefish like Hake or Haddock and call it Scrod, which you can call me, too, if the Glade doesn't work.

Illinois' Unjust 16-Turtle Law

Here's a story illustrative of how creeping authoritarianism is tightening the shackles of regulation in every area of our lives. In Will County, Illinois, State Natural Resources Conservation police spotted a man removing turtles from a pond. Confronting the man, he allowed as how he hunts turtles for his dad, who keeps them in a pond behind his house and likes to watch them. Police followed the suspect's El Camino as he transported three burlap bags containing eleven snapping turtles and five painted turtles to the turtle hunter's residence, and interviewed the father, who showed them his turtle pond and two deep freezers containing turtle meat, which he cooks for his family and gives to friends. The police returned with a search warrant and seized the live turtles and sixty containers of turtle meat, because, it turns out, it is against the law to own more than sixteen turtles in Illinois.

And this is clearly a case of intrusive iron-handed authoritarianism, permitting officers of the state to goosestep, jack-booted, through the backyard fishponds of Illinois, peeping beneath the lily pads for purposes of search and seizure. The wife of the man charged with too many turtles, Carol, was quoted as saying that some people like golf and some like fishing, and her husband catches turtles and has been doing it since he was ten. And I sympathize, because, I, too, grew up with turtles. As my mother had an allergy to pet hair, my childhood domestic animals-of-choice were reptiles and amphibians. My father, as the president of the Lions Club, presided annually over a fund-raising event called the Turtle Derby, at which turtles would be raced for trophies, which is, I suspect, a principally Caucasian sport. And there would invariably be abandoned losers, and they would reside in my turtle pen behind our house and I would maintain a relationship with them, in which, for my part, I fed them and placed them beneath hats to startle visitors to our home when the hats would move across the floor. I never tired of that. And for their parts my turtles would eat lettuce and defecate and die.

   In the ten-year period from 1955 to 1965, I likely buried forty turtles in a herpetological potter's field in the back yard. Archeologists will likely one day ascribe the presence of their skeletal remains to some cult, heretofore unknown. And they will find well preserved examples of the Eastern painted turtle, *Chrysemys picta picta*, and the Northern Diamondback Terrapin, *Malaclemys terrapin terrapin*, and the Eastern Box turtle, *Terrapene carolina carolina*, and the spotted turtle, *Clemmys guttata*, and the snapping turtle, *Chelydra serpentina*, for which the Dyckman boys would troll from a rowboat in Drake's pond. And the big snapping turtles would come up and grab hold of an M-80 and not let go while the Dyckman boys would light the fuse and row like hell. Which did not strike as particularly heinous, those of us familiar with snapping turtles; who knew that if the tables were turned, these vicious prehistoric atavistic embodiments of pure meanness would not hesitate for a moment to do the same thing to us. Anyway, in order to be a nation that can call itself truly free, there should be no limits set on the number of turtles we, as citizens, may acquire.

It was Lord Byron who wrote in "The Bride of Abydos," Canto i, Stanza I.

"Know ye where the cypress and myrtle
Are emblems of deeds that are done in their clime:
Where the rage of the vulture, the love of the turtle,
Now melt into sorrow, now madden to crime," in which he clearly means the turtle to be a metaphor for something or other, and which is further evidence that the only two words which rhyme with turtle are myrtle and fertile, aside from hurdle and girdle and curdle, which don't count because they are "d" words. But as Gamera is my witness, we must resist a tyranny that turns owners of more than sixteen turtles into criminals, because, if the government sends its minions for our turtles, they will surely return for our spiny-tailed iguanas.

Said the Mayo to the Fridge: Close Your Eyes, I'm Dressing

As an individual who takes some measure of pride in the crafting of a classic potato salad which is popular and well received in barbecue circles hereabouts, my attention was engaged by a newspaper clipping I encountered cleaning out a file of old advice columns by Ann Landers, may she rest in peace. "Baffled in Bakersfield," reported that her husband's family never refrigerates the mayonnaise, which stays in the pantry for weeks till the jar is empty despite temperatures of 107 degrees. "Baffled" queried Ann as to why no one gets sick as a result and Ann, in her wisdom, did not endeavor to idly speculate but, rather, redirects the question to the authoritative mayonnaise experts, who are, in this case, the Association for Dressing and Sauces in Atlanta, Georgia.

And I phoned up the Association for Dressing and Sauces to have it confirmed that commercial mayonnaise may be stored at room temperature for quite some time because the acidity from the lemon and vinegar are sufficient to kill bacterial growth, and so it is not the mayonnaise but the other ingredients in potato salad which harbor the sources of food poisoning.

And my conversation with the salad dressings spokesperson in Atlanta produced some interesting facts heretofore unknown to me, such as that mayonnaise has an interesting history, although not as interesting as, say the history of the circus or the history of human-propelled flight.

Mayonnaise is one of the fine Frenchy dressings and sauces included in the "aise," category, such as its snootier cousins Hollandaise and Bernaise. "Aise;" the French word for comfort or ease. The Mayo part derives from the name of the Spanish city of Mahon on the island of Menorca, which is one of the Ballearic Islands to the west of Mallorca in the Mediterranean Sea. In Spanish, the town's name is pronounced Puerto de Mao (mayo); thus; mayo-naise. The reason mayonnaise was invented was as a patriotic tribute to the French victory in the Battle of Mao, which happened in 1756. The island was controlled by the English until, in that year, the grand nephew of French Cardinal Richielieu; Louis-Francois-Armand de Vignerot du Plessis, the Duke de Richelieu, captured the San Felipe fortress and kicked out the British, a victory met with much popular applause. The Duke was a socialite with the Royal Court title of First Gentleman of the Bedchamber, and a renowned party-giver whose eccentricities included inviting his guests to dine in the nude. The Duke's chef is credited with the invention of Mayonnaise as a tribute to the military victory at Mao, and it was a taste sensation as the Rococo period gave way to the Neoclassical prior to the political upheaval in which Europe found the French revolting; as many still do.

And it turns out that the government of the United States of America has become very strict about what constitutes mayonnaise in the years since New York delicatessen owner Richard Hellman first sold his blue ribbon mayonnaise in wooden containers in 1912. The FDA passed a law called the Federal Food, Drug and Cosmetic Act of 1938, to provide for federal "standards of identity," to regulate those who had a notion one could just stick a feather in your cap and call it macaroni. And that Act's Part 169, Subpart B subsection 169.140 (most recently revised in 1977, 1992, and again in 1993), describes mayonnaise as an "emulsified semisolid food prepared from vegetable oil, one or both of the acidifying ingredients specified in paragraph B of this section, add one or more of the egg-yolk-containing ingredients specified in paragraph C of this section, as well as one or more of the ingredients specified in paragraph D. By federal decree mayonnaise must contain not less than 65% by weight of vegetable oil, with lemon or lime juice diluted to an acidity calculated as citric acid of not less than 2 and a half percent by weight. And it continues for many paragraphs in technical detail delineating what must occur before one can call it mayonnaise or risk running afoul of the federal mayonnaise police, who would likely flash their badges and issue a citation to Billy Corgan and inform him that if he is going to use it properly as a song title; according to federal statute subsection 169.140, subsection E; "mayonnaise" has two N's.

Chapter 6—Jokes, Quotes and Verses

Night at the Symphony

As I was sitting in Orchestra Hall Saturday night, listening to composer Elias Tanenbaum's orchestral ode to the bass violin, entitled *First Bassman*, written for his childhood friend Joseph Guastafeste, who has been the principle bassist for the Chicago Symphony Orchestra since the Kennedy-Nixon debates, and wondering, as I often do at Symphony Hall, how they change the light bulbs way up there in the ceiling and thankful that I didn't have to do it---it occurred to me, that, like our show on Saturdays, a Chicago Symphony Orchestra concert is often a "best-of show": this prelude and that interlude and this and that symphonic fragment, in order that, should you desire to hear the entire piece, you are encouraged to obtain the CD at the CSO store next door, where you can also obtain amusing sculptures of bronze monkeys playing instruments.

I have also learned from years of going to the symphony that it should not be assumed that when the orchestra chooses to play Brahms' Symphony Number Two in D Major it was because the first one sucked. Anyway, the program Saturday night was an eclectic mix because the first selection was a contemporary piece, and knowledgeable symphony-goers will know that, by contemporary, we mean "without melody." Most modern composers write pieces which sound like the movie music which starts when the power goes out and the babysitter announces her intention to go down in the basement to see what the trouble is.

But the orchestral star-turn for the bass viol, also known as the double bass or contrabass or bull fiddle, was entertaining and of more than passing interest because it turned out that the composer of the piece was seated right behind me and it is not every day one can meet a classical orchestrator who is still composing, in that the majority of them are decomposing. And I salute Mr. Tanenbaum for providing a work which keeps so many musicians in white bow ties, because it took fully thirty more people to perform his work than the Mozart, during which the bongos languished unattended.

And when one goes to the symphony, it is helpful, for a full appreciation of the event, to know a little something about it, such as that conductor Daniel Barenboim's wife Jackie was a famous cellist who's sex life with Barenboim was described as unfulfilling, and who was given permission by her sister Hilary to have sex with Hilary's husband and who died from MS after running naked through the woods, with Emily Watson in the Oscar-nominated role. So there's that.

And Daniel Barenboim Saturday night performed Mozart's Piano Concerto number 22 in E-flat Major in three movements and when you go to the symphony you have to know where not to clap, because one is only supposed to clap at the conclusion of the concerto, and not between the movements, where the audience is instead expected to hack and cough like a TB ward. And Mr. Barenboim is extremely expressive and several times during the allegro rondo finale he grimaced as is customary when straining to produce a major movement.

And I am always gratified when the program lists a piano concerto in the second half of the performance, because I know during the intermission I can saunter down to the front and watch them bring the Steinway concert grand up the cinderblock elevator shaft right up through the stage because it is quite huge and reminds me of the riddle about what you get when you toss the concert grand piano down the mine shaft and the answer is, "A flat miner." Which is a classic example of classical music humor, as is the one about Arnold Schwarzenegger being offered his choice of Classical composers to portray in a movie, to which he replies, "I'll be Bach."

Immortal Words

Quoting Winston Churchill, "Bartlett's Familiar Quotations is an admirable work," unquote, a quote I found in Bartlett's Familiar Quotations. And while there are those who wish to find themselves, someday, on the cover of the Rolling Stone, I wish to find myself one day within the pages of Bartlett's.

Which I was reminded of as I read about Charles Edward Rushmore, who was a rich New York lawyer at the turn of the century and who died in 1931. It happens that while a youthful attorney of twenty-nine, he was commissioned by New York investors to travel to the Black Hills and secure from tin miners options on their mines. And he visited them on several occasions in 1884 and 1885 and at one point, impressed by a tall and rocky peak rising six thousand feet above a mining camp, he inquired of the rough but kindly miners as to its name, to which one of the miners replied that it had no name but since he asked it would thereafter be forever known thereabouts as Rushmore Peak, and it stuck and thus it is, today, Mount Rushmore. Which, to my knowledge is about the easiest anyone on this planet has ever achieved immortality.

At some times in our lives, especially as we approach an age more than halfway to assuming our duties in the capacity of fertilizer, each of us yearns to have his name preserved in perpetuity for some accomplishment beyond having to pay the stone carver in advance for the inscription. And I concluded long ago that the easiest and least calorie-burning method of securing one's place in the memory of man is to say something sufficiently pithy that others will wish to repeat it. It is the unquoted who are forgotten, the quotable are notable. Studs Terkel is in Bartlett's. The big hardback one. Under the heading, "Studs (Louis) Terkel, 1912 to the present," is the quotation, "Perhaps it is this specter that most haunts working men and women: the planned obsolescence of people that is of a piece with the planned obsolescence of the things they make. Or sell." Unquote. And it matters not if one has the foggiest notion as to his meaning; it will forever be there to be quoted by speechwriters or term paper authors. Bartlett's may stretch the definition of "familiar," when it offers the 15th century German economist Gabriel Biel writing, "Pro tali numismate tales merces," but one is certainly familiar with the translation which is, "You get what you pay for."

And I have yearned to be quotable but can never think of the perfect bromide in my quest for a quality quip. But a light bulb went off when I visited Bartlett's recently to check the source of the phrase "three sheets to the wind," which was attributed to the author of a piece called Life in London, published in 1821, in which the sentence appeared: "Old Wax and Bristles is about three sheets in the wind," and Bartlett's notes it was reiterated by Richard Henry Dana in Two Years Before the Mast in 1840 when he wrote of a character that, "He seldom went up to town without coming down "three sheets in the wind." And suddenly it hit me that one can get into Bartlett's by saying something someone else has already said. Cervantes wrote in Don Quixote; "Honesty's the best policy," while George Washington wrote in his farewell address; "Honesty is always the best policy." Pythagoras spoke of the "music of the spheres," and William Shakespeare wrote of the "Music from the spheres," and Sir Thomas Browne wrote of "maintaining the music of the spheres." Bartlett's Familiar Quotations quotes quoters of quotes. The book is chock-a-block with quoters quoting quotees. Edgar Allen Poe even quotes a Raven.

And so I will aspire to ride piggyback into Bartlett's on the phrase mongering of others, as I have not the ability to speak in golden nuggets that assay out to anything close to 24 carats. I attempt to preserve on a cocktail napkin what I perceive to be a flash of wit in the course of cocktail banter only to awaken to read something to the effect of, "You know what we have lost in the rush to new technology? A good backfire. Without carburetors, where are the backfires of old?" Or, as I said last night at a restaurant, "Good eats. Some living. Huh?" Which is certainly derivative of Benjamin Franklin, who said, "Eat to live, and not live to eat," who borrowed from Moliere who said, "One must eat to live, and not live to eat," who read Plutarch, quoting Socrates, who said, "Bad men live that they may eat and drink, whereas good men eat and drink that they may live." Which is not, technically, stealing because, after all, quoting James Russell Lowell, "Though old the thought and oft expressed, Tis his at last who says it best."

Confessions of a Plagiarist

In the produce section of the grocery store I saw a label on a bin, which said "Russian banana potatoes," and it depressed me to be reminded, again, of how little I know of the world. I have lived half a century ignorant of a vegetable whose name contains the words "Russian," "banana," and "potato."

Who was it that pointed out that some words just never get used together, like "Please saw my legs off," or "Hand me that piano?" I think it was George Carlin. And it turns out you have to be very careful when you quote George Carlin, because I recall the pickle a writer for the Boston Globe got himself into, when he wrote a column and included the line: "Someday I'd love to see the Pope appear on his balcony and give the baseball scores." Almost immediately, somebody pointed out to the newspaper editors that in his recent book, George Carlin wrote, "Someday I wanna see the Pope come out on that balcony and give the football scores." And it could be argued that the two men might have been working to invent the same joke independently, such as when the Duryea Brothers were working on the internal combustion engine simultaneous with Henry Leland and Alexander Winton and several other automobile pioneers on the European continent. Certainly, it cannot be disputed that one version has the Pope delivering the baseball scores from his balcony, while the other has, from the papal balcony overlooking St. Peter's Square, the Pope delivering the football scores, which are undeniably two entirely different sports. But the newspaper bosses demanded the columnist resign for stealing a George Carlin joke that is not even as funny as the one where he said "The day after tomorrow is the third day of the rest of your life."

And lest I likewise face arraignment for aggravated citation without attribution, I will go on record to confess that other people's thoughts have accidentally found their way into my own, just as other people's pens have turned up in my pocket. And there are coffee cups in my office of undetermined ownership. As an individual required to fill a blank computer screen with eight hundred words every day, if I am in the dark as to the identity of the person who defined "Deja Fu" as "the feeling that somehow, somewhere, you've been kicked in the head like this before," should I keep this unattributed remark locked up, or wouldn't the kinder thing to do, and the more generous be, to set it free? Now, most of the time I am scrupulous about giving credit to whom it is necessary to borrow wisdom from for the purpose of appearing clever. But I receive E-mails every day containing unpedigreed quotations such as "So what is the speed of dark?", and "All those who believe in psychokinesis, raise my hand," which would be a shame not to share. Some quotations don't work without knowing who said them; because you have to know it was Steven King when the quote is, "I have the heart of a young boy---in a jar on my desk." But is George Carlin so unmagnanimous as to demand credit whenever the question is "If vegetarians eat vegetables, what do humanitarians eat?", when the author of the equally fine quotation, "If we aren't supposed to eat animals, then why are they made of meat?" remains anonymous.

The clever things said by others are the meat and Russian banana potatoes in a writer's grocery cart, and you can quote me. I am among those who appreciates a well-crafted quotation such as "If a man speaks in the forest and there is no woman to hear him, is he still wrong?" George Carlin. Of course there is an opposing viewpoint among some writers that citing quotations is a crutch used by the creatively crippled, as the drunkard uses the lamppost; for support, rather than illumination, which is something once said by somebody or other. "I hate quotations," Ralph Waldo Emerson was quoted as saying. Ironically.

Findings from the Laughing Academy

When I read the story of how Texas police in Amarillo arrested a man and found eight thousand dollars concealed within his buttocks, several questions arose, the answers to which were not to be found in the news account. Thirty-two year old Carl Meredith was arrested on suspicion of smoking marijuana, and on his person he had fourteen thousand dollars in total; six thousand in his pockets, and between his buttocks, he had hidden away a cache totaling eighty one-hundred-dollar bills.

And to satisfy my own curiosity, I went to the bank and, assuming bills of U.S. currency to be identical in thickness and dimension, no matter the denomination, I obtained a hundred singles, from which I removed twenty. The remaining eighty bills I configured in the following way, to better conceptualize the difficulty in enshrouding their presence from prying eyes within the gluteus cleft. I folded the wad of bills in half, resulting in a mass with the dimensions in inches of three and a half by two and five eighths by 1 inch thick. In other words, the size of two decks of playing cards stacked atop one another. And after some measure of cogitation regarding this incident, I concluded it was funny.

And we all know funny when we see it because funny has been bequeathed to us as a genetic heirloom by our proto-human ancestors out of dusky primordial prehistory. From the first involuntary guffaw from a Homo-sapiens bystander born from a bonked head on a cave door or a stubbed toe on a cave floor, the laugh has been an integral lump in the ethological glob that is human social vocalization.

Which I was reminded of when I read a review in the Journal Nature of the book entitled, "Laughter, a Scientific Investigation," by Robert Provine, a psychology professor at the University of Maryland. And Professor Provine says that in common conversation, laughing manifests itself in a far different way than in comedy. A comedian will often neither smile nor laugh, whereas the audience responds hysterically. But in conversation, it is usually the speaker who laughs more than his listeners, and, in fact, Professor Provine says many speakers attempting to be humorous in social situations laugh 46% more often than their listeners and you know who you are. Provine concludes from his studies that a laugh almost invariably contains the same pattern of syllables, lasts about 75 milliseconds, and is repeated at steady intervals of 210 milliseconds and ends more quietly than it started. Any one laugh involves a single vowel, either a hahahah, or a hohoho; never a ha-ho-ha-ho. And laughing causes laughing, just as yawning causes yawning. Provine suggests a neurological laugh-detector stimulates neurons in the brain triggering more laughs. And by way of example, he recounts an incident in the scientific literature in which an isolated outbreak of laughing and giggling amongst a group of Tanganyikan schoolgirls, in 1962, escalated and spread among their schoolmates, and from thence into the general population, and from there to adjacent communities. The laughing epidemic was so severe it forced the closing of schools and the laughing attack persisted for six months.

Thus, laughing may be described as epidemic, as it is both contagious and infectious, properties known to CBS soundman Charlie Douglass, who invented the TV laugh track machine in 1954 and took it to Desilu Studios to provide a one-man studio audience which would laugh at anything, and he said he got his classic laugh tracks from the audiences at the Burns and Allen radio shows.

In Bombay, India, Dr. Madan Kataria discovered one may eliminate humor altogether and cause laughing by laughing; and has created the Laughing Clubs of India, in which members gather for purposes of therapeutic laughing, meetings at which members build themselves up into a paroxysm of helpless exhaustion. In yoga, this has become known as Hasyayog, and exercises principally consist of Lion Laughing, or laughing out loud; Cocktail Laughing, polite chuckling; or Silent Laughing, holding it in while performing the requisite shoulder shudder. Which is physiologically beneficial, in that laughter lowers blood pressure, increases vascular blood flow, resulting in a lessening of pain, a decrease in stress-causing hormones, and it strengthens immunity and fights infections. On the downside, Indian writer Vilayanur Ramachandran tells, in the medical literature, of a 58-year-old woman patient who was seized by a fit of laughter, which caused her to laugh for two hours, and, despite an injection of morphine, the laugher persisted as noiseless grimaces until she expired from lethal laughing.

Children laugh out loud, on average, 400 times a day. The average adult emits 15 laughs per day, one of which I expended thinking about the fellow with the eight thousand dollars stuffed up his buttocks, because it occurred to me there was another technique he may have employed, rather than folding the 80 bills in half. As uncomfortable an image as that is, it is perhaps preferable to the other configuration, which was to roll up the bills and secure with a rubber band, which I did with my eighty singles; producing a cylinder six inches in circumference and two inches in diameter, or roughly approximating the act of shoving a small can of V-8 Vegetable Juice up one's rectal foyer. Which is funny, when you think about it.

Refuge

As I drove into work this morning I was thinking about how I must come up with a "Last refuge," quotation, in that it was Samuel Johnson who said, "Patriotism is the last refuge of a scoundrel," and it was Salvor Hardin who said, "Violence is the last refuge of the incompetent," and it was Somerset Maugham who said "Art is the last refuge of the ingenious to escape the tediousness of life," and it was Oscar Wilde who said, "Seriousness is the last refuge of the shallow." Of course, it was Oscar Wilde who said, "Action is the last refuge of those who cannot dream," and it was Oscar Wilde who said, "Simple pleasures are the last refuge of the complex," and it was Oscar Wilde who said,

"Consistency is the last refuge of the unimaginative," in that Oscar Wilde had the facility of making up "Last refuge," quotes all the live-long day. And I was thinking that my quote could be, "The Ballet Folklorico is the last Refuge of the Mexican Hat Dance," when I hit a pigeon with my car.

I was coasting toward a parking-garage gate, where a parliament of pigeons is customarily gathered in group discussion, and expected them to part as they always do, when there was a thump and I saw flapping feathers glance off my hood and a pigeon hit the ground and rolled and regained its feet and shook out its feathers and then, as I waited for the garage gate to rise, it lifted its head and shot me the stink-eye. Its unblinking beady black eye was accusatory, in the manner of the eyeball whammy the Italians call *malocchio*, as if to mean, "You don't know the world of trouble you have bought yourself this day," but I returned evil-eye for evil-eye, because it was my position the pigeon had violated the driver-pigeon covenant that it is the pigeon's obligation to remove itself from the motorway and the onus is on the bird to stand in the street with an attitude of invulnerability as though protected by a force field, as though thinking, "Wait for it….wait for it…..wait for…..damn!" And then to flap out of harm's way a nanosecond faster than becoming squab sushi for scavengers.

And I had a sense of déjà vu I had heard this story before, about the unspoken pigeon-driver understanding that birds would always get out of the way, perhaps on Seinfeld. But I couldn't, with certainty, declare this memory to be genuine, which confirms the findings of researchers at Northwestern University, who, for forty years, studied the recollections of males and concluded that, by the time they arrive at middle-age, men have rewritten their youth. High school freshman boys were asked questions about their lives in 1962, and then, at age 48, were asked to recall how they had answered those questions in their youth, and they remembered a lot more family conflict than there was, and a lot less sibling rivalry than there was, and a lot less corporal punishment than there was, and, in fact, answered with the accuracy of somebody who was just guessing. 44% of the men said they would have answered it was okay to have sex in high school, when, in high school, only 15% of them felt that way.

Which gives rise to the metaphysical and philosophical question that if our memory alters our past, is that past false or does it become real, because it is what we remember? Can it be argued that if we remember that Sioux Falls is the capitol of South Dakota, when others suspect that it is Pierre, that we should receive partial credit on the test? Even history as fact is suspect, when we learn that the most memorable sea battle of the Civil War was not between the Monitor and the Merrimac, in that the Merrimac was a sunken federal boat salvaged by the South and its hull used in construction of the Confederate ironclad, the CSS Virginia, which (not the Merrimac), traded shot and shell with the Monitor in Hampton Roads. Ralph Waldo Emerson complained, quoting, "we are shut up in schools and colleges, and recitation rooms for ten or fifteen years, and come out at last with a bag of wind, a memory of words, and do not know a thing." Tom

Stoppard said of our pasts that, "We cross our bridges when we come to them and burn them behind us, with nothing to show for our progress except a memory of the smell of smoke, and a presumption that once our eyes watered."

I suppose it can be said that there is an upside to a Roper poll which shows fewer than one in three college students knows the winning general at the Battle of Yorktown was George Washington. Archeologists will have an easier job of it finding surprising and amazing things to reveal to us about our past, given the majority of us can't remember much past Frasier, season eleven. As New York Times writer Peter Applebome put it, "The next morning our youth was a memory, and our happiness was a lie. Life is like a bad margarita with good tequila, I thought, as I poured some whiskey onto my granola and faced a new day," which I offer, not because it is in any way germane, but because it is a fine quotation, and "Quotations are the last refuge of the uninspired."

From out of the Mouths of Coots

It was when I saw a CNN video clip of the Sheriff of Andrews, North Carolina, interviewed about the years-long manhunt in the wild mountain back-country for a fugitive down south, at the point where he says of that area that "there's rattlers big enough up there to puke up a buck deer," that it occurred to me that the present generation has been negligent in the area of crafting fine rustic sayings. One associates the best vintage regional sayings with the south and with the west, where a cautious investor might be described as "careful as a naked man climbin' a barbed-wire fence."

When I was knee-high to a blackberry bush, there were an abundance of excellent sayings, like "Just because you have a crack in your behind, it doesn't make you crippled," which is what my Uncle Rastus would sometimes say for no discernible reason. We didn't get it, quite, but we all allowed as how it was a fine saying, because, as Uncle Rastus would say, "That's life in the putty knife factory." And there were more good sayings in the 1950s because there were undeniably an abundance of bona fide geezers back in those days.

Today's senior citizens have lost the ability to deliver a quaint aphorism with anything like the skill of a genuine backwoods gaffer, and have to feebly search their inadequately stocked cliché closets and strain to warn you against counting your chickens before they're hatched or cutting your nose off to spite your face, because their maxim and proverb and adage and chestnut cupboards are bare. But when my Uncle Rastus had his hands full, he didn't just have his hands full; he was as busy as a one-eyed cat watching nine rat-holes. Or as busy as a farmer with one hoe and two rattlesnakes. And in fact, if the nation, as a whole, is to receive relief from its idiomatic axiom drought, that relief will likely come from its farmers, because my old Uncle Roy was a farmer and was forever saying things like, "If you were born to be shot, you'll never drown," and "The more you stir the septic tank, the more it stinks." When you missed at horseshoes you "couldn't hit the broad side of a barn with a bass fiddle," and when it was pouring hard outside it was "comin' down like a cow relieving itself on a flat rock." If I told Uncle Roy about the news item about researchers who reported that optimistic people live longer, he would have retorted that "even a blind man on a galloping horse could see that, because it don't take a genius to spot a black goat in a flock of sheep, and it's as plain as a pig on a sofa." After pushing himself away from the Thanksgiving table he'd pronounce himself fatter than a tick on a coon dog and happier than a dead pig in sunshine. And when somebody of his acquaintance wasn't right, he was one fish shy of a full string, or knitting with one needle, or a man whose bale stops short of the hayloft.

So I intend to begin serious study as a geezer in training so that when my boy Jonathan has children of his own, I will have developed enough colorful sayings so as to be not only geezerly but, hopefully, will by that time have become a full blown coot. I say we owe it to a generation yet unborn to have the ability to say, upon the birth of those unborn, that they are prettier than a speckled pup in a red wagon. To be able to say of a political candidate that he could talk under wet cement with a mouthful of Mentadents. To be able to characterize the corporate front office as home to more pricks than a second-hand dartboard.

And if we are to avert losing, as a nation, our ability to age into wizened codgers capable of clicking our teeth and whistling before scratching our necks and mumbling something about a thrifty housewife always peeling the potatoes twice, we have to act now, because it's no good to lock the barn door after the horse is gone. That's like waiting to get that looked at till after the squamous cell has metastasized. That's like burning the crates after the Asian Longhorn Beetle larvae have bored into the Poplars. That's like counting on seeing Bridgette Nielson in Red Sonja before checking to see if it conflicts with Great Chef's of Europe. And pardon me if I stumbled over a couple of phrases back there, but my tongue twisted around my eye teeth and I couldn't see what I was saying.

Rotten Poetry

Poet Thomas Carlyle called poetry, "Musical thought." Gwendolyn Brooks called it, "Life Distilled." Maxwell Bodenheim described it as "The impish attempt to paint the color of the wind." Matthew Arnold called it, The most beautiful, impressive, and widely effective mode of saying things." Which is accurate as a rule, with there being an exception to the rule, which is any poetry by Julia A. Moore, nearly forgotten as the worst poet America has ever produced, and worthy of the highest pejorative, in that, should there exist an antonym for poet laureate, the title would be almost worthy of her.

Her first volume of poetry, "The Sweet Singer of Michigan Salutes the Public," was published in 1876 when she was but 29, and was received with rapturous exultation by the literary elite who considered it the funniest thing they had ever read. Julia Moore's poetry, written in her farmhouse in Edgerton, Michigan, just north of Grand Rapids, dripped with sentimentality and tragedy and fractured meter and forced rhyme; its subject matter often taken from newspaper obituaries.

Reviewing the newly published book, 19th century humorist Bill Nye, wrote of the 36 poems; "Julia is worse than a Gatling Gun. I have counted twenty-one killed and nine wounded in the small volume she has given the public." From the review of the Rochester Democrat: "Shakespeare, could he read it, would be glad that he was dead." The Worcester Daily Press rhapsodized that Julia "reaches for the sympathy of humanity as a Rhode Islander reaches for a quahog, clutches the tendrils of the soul as a garden rake clutches a hop vine, and hauls the reader into a closer sympathy than that which exists between a man and his undershirt."

One example of Ms. Moore's abundant use of the poetical non sequitur is: "Come all good people, far and near, Oh, come and see what you can hear." In her lengthy poem, "William House and Family," she describes in ghastly detail the circumstances regarding this unfortunate family succumbing to smallpox, excerpting:

"They once did live at Edgerton,
They once did live at Muskegon,
From there they went to Chicago,
Which proved their fatal overthrow.
It was William House's family,
As fine a family as you see—
His family was eleven in all,
I do not think it was very small.
Two children died some years ago,
Before they went to Chicago,
Five children there he had with him,
When death his home there enters in."

Her rhyming schemes were often a surprise, as in,
"Remember never to judge people by their clothes, For our brave noble Washington said, "Honorable are rags, if a true heart they enclose," And I found out it was the truth when I got marri-ed."

Happily, for posterity, an anthology entitled "Mortal Refrains: The Complete Collected Poetry, Prose, and Songs of Julia A. Moore, The Sweet Singer of Michigan," is available for 25 dollars from the Michigan State University Press, including the tragic ode to a departed child, "Little Libby," which contains the lines, "While eating dinner, this dear little child Was choked on a piece of beef. Doctors came, tried their skill for a while, But none could give relief." Or her weepy requiem for Hiram Helsel, of whom she wrote, "He was a small boy for his age, When he was five years or so, Was shocked by lightning while to play, And it caused him not to grow." Or her elegy to the newly deceased leader of the Mormons, which begins, "'Tis said that Brigham Young is dead, The man with nineteen wives; The greatest Mormon of the West, Is dead, no more to rise; He left behind his nineteen wives, Forsaken and forlorn; The papers state his death was caused, By eating too much green corn."

Mark Twain included a parody of Julia Moore in Huckleberry Finn, in the character of Emmaline Grangerford, who writes poems inspired by obituaries clipped from the Presbyterian Observer, such as one Huck reads pertaining to a fellow who fell into a well, quoting, "They got him out and emptied him, Alas, it was too late; His spirit was gone for to sport aloft, In the realms of the good and great." Some years ago, a librarian in Flint, Michigan, undertook to memorialize Mrs. Moore by way of an annual poetry competition in which writers presume to emulate the Sweet Singer of Michigan, and, each April, the frightening fruits of this competition are revealed, and posted on the Flint Public Library web site. A personal favorite of mine is the winning poem two years ago by Rudy Espinoza, whose composition reads, in part, "Lets go through the broken streets, the gutters trampled under our feets, meet restless women in the dirt motels of Dort Highway, go get greasy spoon food, eat and not pay, down the streets that open up to discontent. So we look at each other and ask, what the hell is this? Hey, what's that smell?"

Peter Piper Pilots Past Seashell Shoals in Toy Boat

I ran smack into a headline about infighting among ethnic Uzbeks, Tajiks, and Pashtuns which read, "Afghan Factions Fractious," which caused my tongue to drift off onto the lingual shoulder before I regained control of my vocal vehicle. And we, all of us, are vulnerable to hacking through a thicket of verbiage and failing to see the tripwire detonating a phonemic sequence rigged to wrap our tongues so far around our eye teeth we can't see what we're saying.

If Peter Piper picking pickles was the first tongue twister I ever heard, the first one I ever learned was Picky People Pick Peter Pan Peanut Butter, the Peanut Butter Picky People Pick, because it was a commercial and I liked Peter Pan Peanut Butter. In Oaxaca they are taught, "Pepe Pecas pica papas con un pico, con un pico Pepe Pecas pica papas." Which is "Pepe Pecas is chopping potatoes with a pick. With a pick, Pepe Pecas is chopping potatoes." And in Salerno they say, "Il papa pesa al pepe a Pisa; a Pisa pesa il pepe al papa." Which is "The papa weighs the pepper in Pisa. In Pisa, the pepper is weighed by the papa."

And in the course of adolescence I learned about the baby buggy with the rubber bumpers and the toy boat and the seashore shell salesgirl. But it was in a voice training acting course in college that the teacher compelled us to learn, "She stood on the balcony, inexplicably mimicking him hiccupping, and amicably welcoming him in." Then we advanced through, "Betty Botter bought some butter, but, she said, the butter's bitter! If I put it in my batter, it'll make my batter bitter. But a bit of better butter, will make my batter better. So she bought a bit of better butter and it made her batter worse!"

And this exercise was by way of developing articulation, but in my experience developed diction only to the degree one is better able to wrestle fiendish phraseology to the mat in a best of three falls. And, as the gunfighter knows, once having conquered Betty Botter, she is followed by a legion of other challengers, and the day will come when you step into the dusty street and find you are just a hair slower on the draw than Theophilus the Thistle Sifter. He's a way tougher hombre than Moses, who supposes his toeses are roses, and we reckon that Moses supposes erroneously, for nobody's toeses are posies or roses as Moses supposes his toeses to be. Eventually, we acquired the confidence to attempt, "I'm not the fig plucker, nor the fig plucker's son, but I'll pluck your figs till the fig plucker comes." The committed collector is certain to encounter insidious foreign challengers such as "Flyg, fula fluga, flyg! Och den fula flugen flog." Which is Swedish for "Fly ugly fly, fly. And the ugly fly flew." But it isn't the familiar and structured verse such as "I saw Esau kissing Kate. I saw Esau, he saw me, and she saw I saw Esau," that are treacherous, but rather, the unexpected disastrous lingual contortion arising from an accidental encounter with fresh-fried fish fritters, three tree twigs, or a rural brewery. Or when one attempts to say, "This was supposed to be pistachio." And whenever you encounter the words "aluminum" and "linoleum," side by side, cross to the other side of the street without making eye contact.

    The Twister-Master must never become over-confidant, less he become reckless in foolishly attempting "If you're keen on stunning kites and cunning stunts, buy a cunning stunning stunt kite." This should be undertaken only by trained professionals who have achieved a level of competence so as to be able to read Fox In Sox clean through without error. And though my skills have dulled, I can still rise to the bait of a brisk walk through, "Through the thicket of thorns and thistles thumped and thundered and thrashed the thoroughbred of Theo the thief…the thirteen thousand thistles and thorns thrust through the thick of his thigh, thwarting the thoughtless thug.

    But I know, one day, someone better than I will walk through the saloon door and I will know the bullet with my name on it as I hear him speak the challenge,

"Seventy-seven benevolent elephants. Three times. Fast."

Talking the Talk and Knocking the Knock

When I read where the boss at a local country radio station is named Justin Case, it occurred to me that he's one of the very few living Americans who can used his own name in a knock-knock joke. My own name (Knock-knock. Who's there? Dave. Dave who? Dave McBride) is unfit, knockwise. Whereas Justin Case was born to knock.

Which reminds me of something a four year-old of my acquaintance recently said to me. The last time I spoke with him, the lad inquired of me, did I know why the cow had crossed the road? To which I allowed as how, no, I was not in possession of this intelligence, whereupon the precocious pre-schooler answered his own query thusly: to go to the moooo-vies! And commenced to cackling in a most self-congratulatory manner at having put over such a fine jest. And he followed up with other reasons various species of mammals might have for crossing the road, such as sheep going to a baaah-be-cue, or horses wishing to visit their neigh---bors. And I learned it was his Auntie Gayle who introduced him to riddle wordplay and set him on this comedic path, just as it was my own Aunt Emy Lou who said to a three year old me: "Knock knock." And according to protocol I replied, "Who's there?" To which she declared, "Little old lady." Which I naturally followed with "Little old lady who?" And she concluded the exercise, "I didn't know you could yodel," which I took to be the funniest sentenced ever crafted by a human, and which I proceeded to repeat at every opportunity for six weeks minimum.

  And there is something timeless and pure about knock-knock jokes, as they are ritual dialogues in which one individual assumes the fictional persona of a humorous alias, and the other consents to inquire as to the identity of the speaker. And one's first knock-knocks generally involve proper names, such as Wendy, as in, "Wendy red red robin comes bob-bob-bobbin' along." But then one progresses to knock-knock surrealism in which any noun is accepted as a name, such as Chimney, as in, "Chimney isn't breathing, Pinocchio, call 911!" A good, simple, crisply-delivered knock-knock is a pause that refreshes, as contrasted with the commitment of time necessary for a joke that begins, "Bill Gates, the Pope, and Barney the Dinosaur die and go to heaven…" Or one that ends, "…at these prices, it's no wonder." You are not required to have the life experience necessary for the one which goes, "The restaurant menu said I could order breakfast any time. So I ordered French toast during the renaissance." Or the one about French philosopher Rene Descartes sitting alone at the bar at closing time when the bartender asks if he wants last call and Descartes says, "I think not," and suddenly vanishes. Consider how much less cerebral effort is required to enjoy a deftly-delivered; Knock-knock. Who's there? Anita. Anita who? Anita bath. We must waste precious brain-time on a one-liner such as, "Think about how much deeper the ocean would be if sponges didn't grow there." We do not have to think about Justin Case.

Of course, it is only prudent, every once in a while, to be less transparently obvious, as in: Knock-knock. Who's there? Spell. Spell who? W-H-O. Get it? And when next the four year-old humorist engages me in funny fencing and thrusts with his patented "To go the moo-vies," I will parry with a cow allusion of my own where I say, "Knock-knock." And the lad will oblige me with a "Who's there." "Interrupting cow," I will say. And as he begins to recite his next part, I shall interrupt; "Moooo!" Because once in a while, despite its structured formula, there ought to be a surprise.

The old knock-knocks are covered in mold primeval, and so I thought up some new ones today. Knock-knock. Who's there? Adelia. Adelia who? Adelia the cards; Jacks or better to open, sixes wild. Knock-knock. Who's there? Xavier. Xavier who? Xavier your empty excuses for someone who cares. Knock-knock. Who's there? Justice. Justice who? Justice I suspected, it was Moriarty with the venom of the Javanese spitting adder. And lastly: Knock-knock. Who's there? Norma Lee. Norma Lee who? Norma Lee I'd have a fine closing punch line to insert here.

Origin of the Nantucket Bucket

A student of the verse form once divided limericks into three types: limericks to be told when ladies are present; limericks to be told when ladies are absent but clergymen are present; and Limericks. Most would agree with Professor Morris Bishop who wrote:

The limerick is furtive and mean;
You must keep her in close quarantine,

Or she sneaks to the slums
And promptly becomes
Disorderly, drunk and obscene.

In 1846, the modern Limerick verse-style originated with what were then called nonsense rhymes, and Edward Lear published an anthology of them, which was enthusiastically snapped up by no one. However, twenty years later, at its reprint, the British humor magazine Punch seized upon the form and began the fad that had everybody doing them. In the United States, talentless writer but successful copycat Charles Leland used the form as political satire during the civil war. According to limerick scholar G. Legman, who spent years in the collecting of 1700 of the verses in the most extensive anthology of Limericks ever gathered together, cementing his reputation as someone never to invite to a party, the name Limerick was probably applied to the form in the 1880s, after a series of ribald rhymes ending with the chorus, "Won't you come up to Limerick." Even though popularized by the English and the Americans, the metre of the stanzas in the classic five-line Limerick was commonly used in songs in the Irish language throughout the 1700s. But the limerick poetical pattern ending with two short syllables and a long, can be traced back as far as the 1300s. An argument has been made that one of the oldest poems in the English language; "sumer is i-cumen in" contains limerick-like rhythm, thus:

Ewe bleateth after lamb,
Low'th after calve coo;
Bullock starteth
Bucke farteth

Merry sing cuckoo!

Which is what passed for great literature in the dark ages.

But a Limerick barren of at least one word which would catch in the throat of a bishop is not worth the reciting of it. Even if its heart is in the right place, as with:

On the chest of a barmaid in Sale,
Were inscribed all the prices of ale
And on her behind
For the sake of the blind
Was the same information in Braille; or,

There was a young lady in Reno
Who lost all her dough playing Keno
But she made so much Jack
From her work on her back
That now she owns the casino

And I could fashion a verse that passes Federal Communications Commission scrutiny
such as:

A young man from old Bucharest
Had a bull's-eye tattooed on his chest
But, lest he be a target
He'd for two more dinar, get
Tattooed with a bullet proof vest

Which is ultimately unsatisfying, as "old Bucharest" would be far more interestingly paired with breast, or molest, or ingest, or HIV test. Five finely crafted lines of spondaic hexameter with lines three and four generally containing amphibrachs and amphimacers, are still unworthy of the name limerick without the presence of a spoken word violating several federal decency

guidelines. The F-word or the C-word, or the S-word or the one in the verse that goes:
A lass from Kilcornan begat
Three brats, name of Nat, Pat, and Tat
T'was fun in the breeding
But hell in the feeding
When she found there was no tit for Tat
By which, of course, I mean this for that or quid pro quo.

Classic Little Willie

Some things stand the test of time and I'm not only talking about Circus Peanuts. It occurred to me that some things don't hold up over time, as I watched the movie West Side Story, where the music is still stirring but the portrayal of gang activity seems a trifle quaint.

On the other hand, a literary work which seems, to me, as fresh today as when I first encountered it, is the anthology of Little Willie Poetry I have assembled over the years. I find it therapeutic to distract myself from the distressing headlines reflective of our times, by leafing leisurely and affectionately through my collection of Little Willie Poems. Because, unlike West Side Story, with its romanticized portrayal of gang-bangers as tragic heroes, Little Willie stands the test of time for it's content, which, at its core, is pure unvarnished meanness.

For mindless cruelty, no poet has yet bested or overmastered the anonymous author of the verses which are the distillation of unredemptive inhumanity; which began in the last century with Old Little Willie Number

One, "Willie saw some dynamite, Couldn't understand it quite, Curiosity seldom pays, It rained Willie seven days," and continued through the dead sister series, "Little Willie, mean as hell, Tossed his sister in the well, Mama said, while drawing water, "Gee, it's hard to raise a daughter." Or another in the same genre: "Little Willie, feeling mean, Pushed his sister through a screen, Mother stopped his innovations, Said it made for strained relations."

And no Willie Anthology is complete without, "Willie with a thirst for gore, Nailed his sister to the door. Mother said with humor quaint, "Willie dear, don't scratch the paint." Or "Willie made a guillotine, And on it slew his sister Jean. Said mother, coming with the mop, These messy games must simply stop."

And there is the dead-baby series, like "Willie bashed open baby's head, To see if brains are gray or red, What a naughty boy is he, He shall have no jam for tea." Another classic of the genre goes, "Willie, I regret to state, Cut the baby up for bait. We miss her when it's time to dine, But Willie's fish taste simply fine."

But despite Willie's steadfast dependable homicidal amorality, there is intrinsic justice in the Willie series because, most often, it is Willie himself whose life exists only to be extinguished as a macabre punchline. By way of illustration: "Willie fell down the elevator, Wasn't found till six days later, Then the neighbor's sniffed, "Gee whiz," What a spoiled child he is." And after I recently shared the verse where "Little Willie was a chemist. Little Willie is no more. For what he thought was H2O, Was H2SO4," (in which Little Willie expires from drinking sulfuric acid), I was E-mailed two more Little Willies to add to my collection.

The first is a rare two-verse Willie to which E-mailer Lela May adds the parenthetical historical factotum that mirrors used to be backed with mercury: "Little Willie from the mirror, Licked the mercury off, Thinking in his childish error, It would cure his whooping cough. At the funeral, Willie's mother, Smartly said to Mrs. Brown, "'Twas a chilly day for Willie, When the mercury went down." And the second is from Duncan Speece, whose offering goes, "Willie in a rage insane, Threw his head beneath a train, All were quite surprised to find, How it broadened Willie's mind."

Which, you'll agree, holds up just fine. As contrasted with West Side Story, which delivers the wrong message to young impressionable minds who will come away from it believing the principal activity of street gangs is choreography.

Wrecking Emily Dickinson

I was gathering books to give away to make room for more when I came across poems by Archie Ammons. I liked Archie Ammons because he started writing poetry during World War II in the South Pacific when he was a sailor like my dad. He was on the USS Gunason and my dad was on the Birmingham and once, after Archie Ammons got famous, my dad said, "It says here he was on the Gunason. I knew the Gunason," because that was what ex-sailors said.

And I was given a book of poetry by Archie Ammons which I liked because the poems were short, such as one called Late November, which goes, "The white sun, like a moth on a string circles the south pole." The end. Or one called "Coward," which goes, "Bravery runs, in my family." Of course to become famous he had to write longer pieces dripping with profundity like the one where he went looking for the lowly so as to have something by which to measure his own significance and the poems ends, "...though I have looked everywhere, I can find nothing lowly in the universe: moss, beggar, weed, tick, pine, self, magnificent with being!"

A.R. Ammons wrote stuff like, "The quickest way to change the world is to like it the way it is," and he wrote on a typewriter that printed out his longer poems on a single continuous strip of paper. And he used mostly lower-case letters and employed the colon as his favorite all-purpose punctuation, because, he said, the colon fairly promised there would be something before it and after it.

And speaking of the colon; I also liked Archie Ammons because even though he won the Robert Frost Medal and the National Book Award and the National Book Critics Circle Award and the Library of Congress Prize for Poetry and the MacArthur Foundation genius grant, he is also the poet who wrote a poem, the reading of which, in its entirety, on the radio, would result in an FCC fine in the hundreds of thousands, in which the word shit appears ninety times, not including the title. And it does appear in the title, and the title is "Shit-List; or, Omnium-gatherum of Diversity into Unity." And it begins, quoting, "You'll rejoice at how many kinds of Shit there are:" at which he commences a poetical shopping-list of fecal effluvium, including that passing through the gosling, the rainbow trout, the elephant, (the discharge from which he describes as "awesome as process or payload,"); the caterpillar, "so many dark kinds, neatly pelleted as mint seeds); the robin, "that oozes white down lawn chairs"; and he invites the reader to consider the amazing diversity of BM including the evacuations from the chicken, pelican, dog, cricket, elk, shrew, whale, weasel, gazelle, baby rhinoceros, magpie, bat, otter, macaque, gooney bird, alpaca, seahorse, python, peccary, buffalo and baboon." This odiferous ode appears in the poetry anthology I came across, in which his date of birth is listed as 1926, followed by a dash, and no end date, as though the book believes him to be alive, which, inside its covers, he remains, though he died in 2001.

Which I offer as a public service for lovers of poetry. And to provide balance, as a public service to haters of poetry, I offer a sure-fire way of ruining Emily Dickinson for everybody, forever. Dickinson, of course, was the shy, brooding, Massachusetts maid who wrote terse lines like these:

I felt a funeral, in my Brain,
and mourners to and fro
Kept treading, treading, till it seemed
That Sense was breaking through
And when they were all seated,
A service like a Drum—
Kept beating—beating—till I thought
My mind was going numb.

And she wrote primarily in the form of a quatrain with three iambic feet, which, it turns out, is the same as,

"The Yellow Rose of Texas." Thus, virtually all of Emily Dickinson's poems can be sung to "The Yellow Rose of Texas." (Re-read above to the tune of The Yellow Rose Of Texas.)

Or you might put this one to the test: "This is my letter to the World---That never wrote to me---The simple News that Nature told---With tender Majesty---Her Message is committed---To hands I cannot see---For love of Her, Sweet countrymen---Judge tenderly of me." Or the famous "There is no frigate like a Book---To take us lands away---Nor any Coursers like a Page---Of prancing poetry---This Traverse may the poorest take---Without oppress of Toll---How frugal is the Chariot---That bears the human soul." Works with every one.

Chapter 7—Mark Your Calendar

January 29: Claudine Longet's Birthday

I was entertaining the notion of taking today off as a holiday, the 29th of January being Claudine Georgette Longet's 61st birthday. I was in love with Claudine Longet before she became the O.J. Simpson of the 70s and before Saturday Night Live ran video of downhill skiers with a background of gunshots and Jane Curtin turned to Chevy Chase to say, "Uh oh. He seems to have been accidentally shot by Claudine Longet." I wish I could have been there for her, in Aspen, to let her mascara run onto my Merino wool Irish cardigan. Because Claudine Longet made you want to take care of her. I was in love with Claudine Longet before I knew she was married to Andy Williams.

Claudine met Andy Williams in Las Vegas where she was an 18-year-old dancer in the Folies Bergere, and he was a 34 year-old TV star. The year was 1960. Andy Williams' official version of their meeting was this: He was walking to his hotel when he encountered Claudine fretting over her stalled car. As their eyes met, into his memory returned images of the pretty child of eight or nine he always saw roller skating on his trips to Paris to visit the Louvre; the beautiful little girl who lived near the Pont Neuf. Now, miraculously, she was here, a woman fully grown, and neither would argue with destiny. It was a better story for the publicist to run with than "Thirty-something straight-arrow crooner acquires sexy arm-charm Vegas showgirl a shade over half his age." The year they wed, Andy Williams recorded Moon River. Andy's power in show business got Claudine into TV.

She drifted through a dozen sixties TV shows, reprising time after time her signature role as the beautiful waiflike French girl with the wide eyes. She appeared in "McHale's Navy" in the role of Yvette Gerard, and reappeared in the "McHale's Navy" movie two years later as Andrea Bouchard. She appeared twice in the series, "Combat;" once as Babette, and other as Claudette. She was Suzanne in "Twelve O'clock High," and Marianne in "Rat Patrol." She appeared as Michelle Monet, on "Alias Smith and Jones," shortly before star Peter Deuel was found shot to death in his apartment, a suicide. In 1965, playing Ben Gazarra's girlfriend in an episode of "Run For Your Life," she sang the Antonio Carlos Jobim song, "Meditation," which landed her a contract to do an album with Herb Alpert's A&M records. That record, titled, "Claudine," came out in 1967, just in time for me to obtain it for my portable record player in my dorm room at Ohio University. During breaks from The Moody Blues and The

Temptations and The Beatles, we mesmerized guys fantasized over the big-eyed living lost-waif Keane painting as she covered sixties pop hits with sexy-breathy sugar, pretending to be unaware she was driving men mad. In her best Hollywood role, she appeared as the quintessential 60s party girl in Blake Edward's 1968 Peter Sellers movie, "The Party," featuring more go-go boots than an Austin Powers cattle call.

In 1972, she met a skier at a race in Bear Valley, California. A world-class pro skier at the top of his game. He was Vladimir Sabich, whose friends called him Spider. Their attraction was atomic, and their relationship was volatile. There was the time Spider was having beers and conversation with a pal at a café when a wine glass sailed across the room and hit him in the chest and shattered to the floor, at which Spider turned to his pal and said, "I think Claudine wants to talk to me." But he moved the ethereal chanteuse into his Aspen chalet. She and Andy Williams went separate ways in 1975, Claudine going her way with 2.5 million of Andy's savings. On a gray day in March of America's Bicentennial, Claudine tired early of skiing and retired to Aspen's Center Bar where she spent the afternoon in the company of white wine. She got home at four, just before Spider arrived back from the slopes. Preparing to shower, he had stripped to his blue thermal underwear when Claudine appeared with his imitation German luger .22 caliber pistol. Was she homicidal? Was he showing her how it worked? Were they roughhousing and joking? Only two people knew and one of them is only reachable via séance.

The night she shot Spider, Claudine stayed over at John Denver's house. And the airport stayed open late for Andy Williams. In testimony at the trial, they said Spider had grown tired of Claudine and had told her to move out. The prosecution called her an over-the-hill ex-ingénue about to be dumped by a younger lover. Claudine was 34. Spider was 31. But the jury didn't buy reckless manslaughter and convicted her of negligent homicide. She could have gotten 2 years. The judge gave her thirty days in the county jail, which she served following her return from a vacation in Mexico. She began dating her defense attorney, who left his family to marry her, and they live together in Aspen, where Spider Sabich memorabilia is still on view in a framed display case at the Hard Rock Cafe. I wonder how she looks on the threshold of acquiring a senior discount card. Is she still a wispy doe-eyed delicate French confection with an appealing lisp? Is she happy? The Chicago Punk band Geezers put it this way in their pounding rock ballad, "Whatever Happened to Claudine Longet?" as they sing; "Alpine frolic in the snow, white on white, too much blow, Spider told her she had to go, She pulled a gun, he said, 'Oh, no!' We all know the old adage. Claudine just wanted a love that was average. Dead the handsome Spider Savage. His head looked like exploded cabbage. No more Williams Family Christmas joys. No Bowie Duets, no Drummer Boys. Claudine's in jail, she's lost her toys. Does she still have that beautiful voice?"

Geezers guitarist Joe Hova says every time he plays the Claudine Longet song in a club, he offers a prize to anyone who knows who she was or what ever happened to her. And nobody's ever won.

February: How to Be Like George

President's Day is George Washington's fake birthday, which is really the 22nd, eleven days after the commemoration of Abraham Lincoln's natal day. And though Lincoln was born in Kentucky, his family moved him to Illinois at an early age when they learned his name was on all the license plates. Young Abe Lincoln grew up to become a beloved American icon despite the enormous handicap of having been a lawyer.

And many believe President's Day combines Washington's and Lincoln's Birthday, but in the text of the Monday Holiday Law of 1968, it specifically mandates that this day celebrate Washington's birthday and no other. Though it has become known generically as President's Day, as recently as 1998 Congress rejected a bill to rename the public holiday called "Washington's Birthday," "President's Day," because it would elevate our worst presidents---including James Buchanan, chosen worst among historians in a C-Span poll; Warren Harding, voted worst in a Chicago Sun-Times poll; and Franklin Pierce, U.S. Grant, Richard Nixon, Zachary Taylor, and Millard Fillmore, by presidential scholar Robert Ferrell---to equality with the best. So today remains a tribute to a single president, George Washington, who was, by all accounts, a striking man, standing 6 feet 2 in stocking feet and weighing a buff 175 in his prime, broad of shoulder, and muscular from farming his estate, a sinewy slab of colonial beefcake tartare. He excelled at horsemanship, billiards, card playing and wrestling.

But, to his greatness, historians may ascribe no better explanation than a list copied in his own hand into a notebook while a boy; a list of the 110 Rules of Civility. French Jesuits composed the rules in the late 1500s, and they were translated into English as a volume entitled, "Youths Behavior, or Decency in Conversation Amongst Men." George Washington copied these rules and memorized them, and titled them, "The Rules of Civility and Decent Behavior in Company and Conversation," and I have a copy in my bookcase and offer the following short list, as relevant today as when the founding fathers were able to enter Colonial Williamsburg without having to sit through the orientation film.

"When in company, put not your hands to any part of the body not usually discovered." "In the presence of others, sing not to yourself with a humming noise, or drum with your fingers or feet." "If you cough, sneeze, sigh, or yawn, do it not loud but privately; and speak not in your yawning, but put your handkerchief or hand before your face and turn aside." "Sleep not when others speak." "Put not off your clothes in the presence of others." "Spit not into the fire, nor set your feet upon the fire, especially if there be meat before it." "Shift not yourself in sight of others, nor gnaw your nails." "Bedew no man's face with your spittle by approaching too near him when you speak." "Kill no vermin as fleas, lice, ticks, et cetera, in sight of others. If you see any filth or thick spittle, put your foot dexterously upon it, or if it be upon the clothes of your companions put it off privately." "When you see a crime punished, you may be inwardly pleased, but always show pity to the suffering offender." "If you deliver anything witty and pleasant, abstain from laughing thereat yourself."

And according to historian Richard Brookhiser, Washington was seen to laugh in public once (and that was at the theater at a joke at his own expense) but was himself quite witty. By way of example; as he presided over the Constitutional Convention of 1787, when it was proposed that the national standing army be limited to 3,000 men, he was heard to say, as an aside, quoting, "Then we should have another article providing that no foreign nation with an army exceeding 3,000 men be allowed to invade." An illustration that Washington's wit was as wry and dry as was Jefferson's and Lincoln's. And well we might ask, where are the Lincolns and the Jeffersons and the Washingtons of today? A question, to which, the late Pat Paulsen once replied---"In the NBA."

March 16: St. Urho's Day

Today is March 16th and the time is upon us once again to celebrate the memory of perhaps the patron saint of drinking occasions and I am speaking, of course, of Saint Urho.

For non-Finns unacquainted with St. Urho, he was made up in 1956 by the manager of the Ketola Department Store in Virginia, Minnesota, home of the World's Largest Floating Loon, half way between Duluth and International Falls, about fifty miles from the Canada border as the crow flies, or 85 miles if the crow follows route 53. And this department store manager, by the name of Dick Mattson, was consuming alcoholic beverages at a St. Patrick's Day party and declared to the gathering that St. Urho (pronounced OOOOR-hoe) had it all over St. Patrick. And when his companions confessed their ignorance of particular holy good egg, Mr. Mattson proclaimed him to be the patron saint of Finnish vineyard workers, by virtue of driving the poisonous frogs out of Finland, and further embellished St. Urho's legend with expansive tales of his miraculous achievements. And the inhabitants of northern Minnesota, where the winters are long, embraced the legend of St. Urho as a felicitous cause for celebration and justification for intoxication in a double-dose of drinking in tandem with the Irish patron's day. And department store co-worker Gene McCavic composed a legend in the form of an Ode to a boy named Urho who obtained his super-strength from a diet of fish soup and sour milk. As the legend spread across Minnesota, a Finnish college professor named Sulo Havumaki revised the story thusly:

Before the last glacial period, when wild grapes were abundant in the fertile fields of Finland, the grapes were threatened by a plague of giant grasshoppers. We know this from ancient pictograms etched into the thighbone of an extinct giant bear. The boy who would be saint, Urho, stood in the grape fields and shouted, in a voice described as "splendid and loud," "Heinasirkka, heinasirkka, menae-taalta hiiteen," which means, "Grasshopper, grasshopper, go away." This spell drove the grasshoppers into the sea, saving the wine crop. For this reason Urho is the patron saint of Finnish grape growers, of which there are presently none.

In the 1970s, the Minnesota town of Menahga, which is Chippewa for "blueberry," commissioned an artist to carve St. Urho from a one-ton block of oak, but the woodcarver is reputed to have taken the money and vanished. In 1982, the town fathers gave the oak block to itinerant chainsaw sculptor Jerry Ward, who crafted a 12-foot figure of the saint, clutching a pitchfork skewering a giant grasshopper, which stands on the east side of U.S. Highway 71, about 40 miles from Bena, home of Minnesota's only restaurant inside a fish. Actually, the St. Urho statue tourists get their pictures taken with today is a fiberglass replica, the original being so highly thought of it is sheltered from the weather, locked up in the mausoleum in the Menahga cemetery.

It is too late for one to get up there for the big St. Urho's dance tonight at the VFW Hall, but there's still time to make the parade tomorrow, which steps off at one, followed by ice golf on Spirit Lake. Take route 12 out of Minneapolis, through Darwin, home of the World's Largest Ball of Twine, and turn north on route 71. Menahga is but a half-hour drive from Nevis, home to the World's Largest Tiger Muskie; Hackensack, home to the giant statue of Paul Bunyan's Girlfriend; and Pequot Lakes, home of the World's Largest Fishing Bobber.

So, this evening, let us lift a glass and speak the words of Gene McCavic and Richard Mattson, who composed the definitive Ode to St. Urho, which goes, "Ooksie kooksie coolama vee--Santia Urho is the poy for me. He chase out the hoppers as pig as birds. Neffer pefore haff I heard dose words. He really told those bugs of green. Bravest Finn I effer seen. Some celebrate for St. Pat unt hiss snakes--But that Urho boy got what it takes. He got tall and strong on feelia sour--And ate culla moyakka effery hour. Tat's why da guy could chase dose beetles. What crew was thick as jack pine needles. So let's give a cheer, in our best way, On this sixteenth of March, St. Urho's Day!"

The original text of this Ode to St. Urho was written by hand on a piece of wrapping paper, and is now on display at the "Iron World Museum," in Chisholm, Minnesota, eighteen miles from Eveleth, home of the World's Largest Hockey Stick.

April 30: Vappu Day Eve

The Internet is a wondrous thing which has the power to teach the inhabitants of the planet that we are more alike than we imagine and not only in our shared desire to seek out doctored photographs of nude celebrities. We can learn much about other fraternal chapters in the brotherhood of man, and I am speaking specifically of Vappu Day.

Tomorrow, May first, is Vappu Day in Finland, a national holiday unfamiliar to me until I chanced upon a Vappu Day Internet site several years ago, which was a revelation to me, as it will surely be, I believe, to you. It turns out Vappu is a corruption of the name of the Catholic Saint Walpurgis, whose feast day is tomorrow and whose name got mixed up with the German fertility goddess Waldborg, and who has become known in Europe as the patron saint of witches, in a mixing of Catholicism with paganism, because the holiday goes way back before Christianity hung up a shingle and opened for business in Europe. And Walpurgis in

Scandinavian is pronounced Valborg, and in Finland they call it Vappu. There, the holiday goes back to the Vikings, and was a festival to celebrate the return of spring. But there is a darker meaning to Vappu, because it is exactly six months from Halloween. The ancient Finns believed that All-Hallow's Eve was the last day the evil spirits, and hobgoblins, and imps, could make mischief, before winter forced them to withdraw back into the bowels of the earth until spring.

And tonight is Vappu Eve, the night when the goblins spring back out from inside the earth to play pranks on mortal men for another six months, an event requiring Vappu celebrants to engage in general debauchery, especially right after midnight. Other cultures celebrate the holiday, but it is the Finns who invented the peculiar traditions which transform Vappu into an event, compared to which, a Chicago St. Patrick's day is a tea party at Bible school.

When you graduate from high school in Finland, you get a cap like the one the Skipper wore on Gilligan, only white. When you get to college, each university faculty has its own official color, and students buy overalls in the faculty colors. These overalls are like the jumpsuits the pit crew wears at the Indy 500. These are called your party overalls. When you party, you wear your white cap and your party overalls. In addition, each party club has its own special patch sewn on its party overalls, and partiers are encouraged to mingle to collect and trade patches, and so it gives men and women who are strangers to each other an automatic excuse to strike up alcohol-lubricated conversations to negotiate the trading of patches for their party overalls, which can involve sex. Some Finns even go so far as to carry with them small knives with which to surgically remove portions of their party overalls—a leg...a sleeve...a pocket---and swap those so as to assemble amazing Technicolor party overalls.

And as they begin to drink champagne at the stroke of 6pm Finland time on Vappu Eve, in addition to patches, they love to swap jokes about the Swedes, like, "The Russians have a simple way to sink Swedish subs. They send a diver down to knock on the hatch." Or, "Did you see the headline where Swedish mountaineer Christer Olsson, has failed again in his attempt to climb over the sound barrier?" Or, "a Norwegian and a Swede were competing to see who could lean furthest out of a window, when suddenly, the Swede won." And they laugh at themselves, too, with lines like, "Did you hear about the Finn who loved a woman so much he almost told her?" For those fortunate enough to have access to the Internet, a search of the word Vappu will lead one to all manner of personal web pages of Finns who maintain them for the purpose of displaying photographs of themselves irretrievably and thoroughly wasted on Vappu Day, glassy-eyed, clad in their patch-covered party overalls, their smiling faces studies in cataleptic tranquility in the bliss of total Vappu immersion.

So tonight, Finland puts on its party overalls, on an evening, upon which, virtually the entire adult population of the nation is expected—even encouraged—to get drunk, which they will proceed to do with a national zeal. And then, after a night of hedonistic drinking and joking and singing and sex, they all have hash for breakfast before noon and go home to bed and sleep all day till evening when they all go out for dinner and start drinking again without their party overalls but still wearing their caps. Round trip to Helsinki from O'Hare; Scandinavian Airlines; $1,820 round trip.

June: Father's Day Memories of Tarzan

Every Father's Day I think about Tarzan, because my dad never suffered any other Tarzan than Johnny Wiesmuller. I would tolerate a Buster Crabbe or a Lex Barker or a Jock Mahoney, but Dad would sooner turn compost rather than sit still for an ersatz Tarzan. Every Saturday afternoon when I was a boy playing Boy to dad's Tarzan, Tarzan Theater would come on TV to a background of jungle drums and dad on the couch and I on the floor would watch old Tarzan movie adventures in darkest Africa which my dad was enlightened enough to instruct me was so named because of its untracked remoteness and not because of the pigmentation of its inhabitants.

And lest we forget, the legend of the Great White Ape was born, not in the remote vastness of the dark continent, but in an apartment in Chicago just two blocks west of where the Bulls play today. Edgar Rice Burroughs supplemented his income while manager and advertising copywriter for a pencil sharpener company, by writing stories for pulp magazines, and a well-received sci-fi piece called "Under the Moons of Mars" encouraged him to write fiction full time. And he wrote the first Tarzan story in 1912 and it was so popular as a magazine story he was offered a book contract and

Tarzan of the Apes was published in 1914; the first of 25 books about the infant son of Lord Greystoke and Lady Alice, abandoned in the African jungle and raised by apes; and few remember that the original Tarzan of the Apes ends in Wisconsin.

And in 1918 Hollywood filmed Tarzan of the Apes starring Elmo Lincoln, who was the goofiest-named Tarzan till Herman Brix who was the goofiest-named Tarzan till Caspar Van Dien. And Edgar Rice Burroughs moved out west to oversee the making of Tarzan movies, and bought a big ranch near Hollywood, which he named Tarzana, which became the name of the town that grew up around it.

And we learned many things, dad and I, from Tarzan (who was the first anti-gun activist who would always smash the thunderstick of some minor character whom, it would turn out, didn't need it anyway when he vanished beneath the quicksand)---such as that Tarzan could speak the language of Kerchak the Ape, and Tantor the Elephant and Numa the Lion, but Cheetah would have to interpret for the benefit of the rhinos and wild pigs and there was just no talking to the reptiles. And Johnny Weismuller could kill any jungle beast armed only with a knife. As kids we wondered why he never had to wipe off his knife, and Glen Orcutt said it was because if the movie showed the blood the girls in the audience would faint which would require them to stop the movie while the ushers brought smelling salts, because girls in old movies were forever requiring smelling salts.

And my dad and I would lean forward expectantly when the savage Mbongos tied the captured safari bearers to the bent saplings because we knew that with a leg tied to one bent-over tree and the other leg fastened to a tree straining in the opposite direction, the result when they severed the rope was why they had to cut to the faces of the next-in-line, who would grimace as though they'd tasted some milk way past its expiration date, just before Tarzan had the elephants stomp the village. And Mia Farrow's mother, Maureen O'Sullivan, was a much more desirable Jane than Bo Derek even with her clothes on, although we preferred it when she wore her leather bikini. And Boy was Johnny Sheffield who grew up to become Bomba the Jungle Boy.

And my dad would be disappointed if Tarzan Theater substituted a Lex Barker or a Gordon Scott, or, worse still, a Bomba the Jungle Boy; but although a Tarzan purist, he would stay and watch if Tarzan Theater played a Jungle Jim movie, because Jungle Jim was still Johnny Wiesmuller; just too old for the loincloth, though he could still wrestle a rubber crocodile.

Dad left to join Johnny Wiesmuller up on the escarpment prior to the most recent Tarzan treatment, which was the Disney cartoon; Hollywood Tarzan movie number 52, but it had jokes and songs so he would have been scornful of it, as he took his Tarzan seriously.

But again, each Father's Day I think about Tarzan, Lord of the Jungle, King of the Apes, and arguably the last white dude to throw a scare into a crowd of black people just by hollering at them. And I pause for a moment to send a message up to The Escarpment; a message that Boy says hi.

July 21: Hemingway's Birthday

I was unlucky enough to have been in the seventh grade when Ernest Hemingway died from natural causes in Ketchum, Idaho, as his father had also died from lead poisoning, as did his brother Leicester.

It was the summer of 1961 and the Junior High English teachers had already locked in their curriculum for that fall. But the following summer, English instructors, mindful that America's foremost literary laureate had eaten a shotgun shell, began changing the curriculum, and out went *The Red Badge of Courage* and *A Tale of Two Cities*, and in came *For Whom the Bell Tolls* and *The Snows of Kilamanjaro*, and by September of 1963, junior high freshmen across this land returned to class to hear for the first time, the dozen most terrifying words of High School English: "A Farewell to Arms, and In Love and War; compare and contrast." I was just shy of 15. My heaviest reading thus far had been, *The Secret of the Old Mill*, starring Frank and Joe Hardy, sons of renowned detective Fenton Hardy and chums to Chet Morton. A fine starting line for a lifetime of reading, for, as a literary writer once pointed out, the Hardy boys books introduced generations of greenhorn readers to the adverb. Joe and Frank and Chet and Iola never said anything. Rather, they chortled, murmured, gasped, muttered, mused and, upon occasion, ejaculated.

Ernest Hemingway did not write *To Have And Have Not* for an individual who maintained a subscription to Uncle Scrooge and streamers on his handlebars. But we read as much Hemingway as the English teachers could cram into four years which caused us to resent Hemingway in our conviction that, had he not selfishly elected to end his life so abruptly, we'd still be reading Booth Tarkington and James Fennimore Cooper. And when the assignment was to report on our favorite Hemingway book, mine would always be *The Old Man and the Sea* because it was far and away the shortest.

But over the years I picked up enough Hemingway lore (The Ritz Bar, Sloppy Joes, his Key West cats' six-toed descendants) that, on a visit to Mexico, I went to a bullfight for the purpose of understanding Hemingway's passion for it, which I failed to do, in that it bore little resemblance to *Death in the Afternoon* or *The Sun Also Rises*. Rather, my bullfight began with the Dos Equis bikini girls dancing to recorded Ricky Martin and shooting logo T-shirts into the stands, followed by spectators chosen out of the audience to chase goats and caballeros twirling ropes. Then the bull came in looking mean enough but it did not go well in that it kept charging the pointy-stick people on the horses instead of the matador. And later, when it had been thoroughly stuck like a pincushion and bloodied, it knocked the matador down and gouged him in the shoulder with a horn and walked across him before the matador jumped up and dared a few more passes before sticking the long sword into El Toro's spine. That was supposed to end it, but it went wrong and the spectators hooted and booed and the bull was still twitching when the horses dragged him out and it was altogether a non-glorious Hemingway afternoon.

And out of respect for Ernest Hemingway I will decline to celebrate what would have been his birthday today because it is clear as Idaho spring-water he sure as shootin' himself didn't wish to celebrate it his own self. And it cannot be argued that there is something genetically self destructive about the Hemingways as was demonstrated by the gunshot suicides of the Hemingway brothers Ernest and Leicester and their father, by the drug overdose suicides of Ernest's sister Ursula and granddaughter Margeaux, and by the decision of Mariel Hemingway to appear in the 1996 movie, Bad Moon, history's worst werewolf film in which the actor cast as her brother lurks malevolently and sweats and grimaces and might as well have werewolf tattooed on his forehead whilst Mariel remains oblivious to the cause of everyone around them turning into shredded wheat.

August 4: Burkina Faso National Day

On my Georgia O'Keefe calendar with the painting of the calla lilies (which strikingly resembles the secret Victoria keeps), it says that today is National Day in Burkina Faso, an African nation slightly larger than Colorado.

It was on this day in the year 1983 that Captain Blaise Compaore staged a military coup that overthrew the officers who had overthrown the elected government in a military coup, and changed the name of the country from Upper Volta, which was for years the virtual definition of geographic obscurity. In the intervening years since its revolution, Burkina Faso has been transformed, from an unknown remote landlocked economically depressed backwater of Central West

Africa, into an unknown remote landlocked economically depressed parliamentary dictatorship in Central West Africa.

Actually, it is no longer a dictatorship, Captain Blaise Compaore having been elected president, in 1991, by an overwhelming 90% of the 25% of the citizens who actually voted. I undertook to find out more about Burkina Faso by turning to the Worldwide Web site maintained by the Central Intelligence Agency, which offers information about the nations of the world to any citizen. So much information does the CIA web site have on the nation of Burkina Faso, you'd almost think they had somebody spying on them.

Among the facts: Burkina Faso is a signatory to the Law of the Sea treaty, ironically not having access to the sea by virtue of being landlocked, and a signatory to the Nuclear Test Ban Treaty, ironically not home to any nuclear scientists by virtue of four out of five Burkinabes being unable to read or write and having a fleeting acquaintance with money and food. The average wage earner in Burkina Faso makes the U.S. equivalent of 700 dollars a year, which relieves them of the pressure of having to deal with either the cable company or the Internet.

Major cities in Burkina Faso are Bobo-Dioulasso, which would be a fine name for a professional wrestler, Ouahigouya (oowa-higooya), which I will suggest to my boy Jonathan as a fine name for a rock band, and its capitol, Ouagadougou, the world's most enjoyable-to-pronounce city.

To confirm my facts, I phoned the Burkina Faso embassy in Washington D.C., and was informed by the

Burkinabe intern (Burkinabe being the adjective which describe one who is a Burkina Faso-ite), that, aside from herself, the embassy was empty, because of the national holiday. She was able to tell me that the meaning of the words, Burkina Faso, translates to "People of Integrity", and that would, I am certain, be descriptive of everyone in the Burkina Faso government, from Prime Minister Kadre Desire Ouedraogo, to the Ambassador, Gaetan Ouedraogo, to the economic counselor, Souleymane Ouedraogo, to the Financial Attache, Boureima Ouedraogo.

The person with whom I spoke was a delightful young woman with a lilting British-African accent, who said to call her Twitty, and to whom I did not disclose that the CIA website predicts her life expectancy to be forty-two. And so this evening, I will lift a glass and join all the citizens of Burkina Faso in their celebration of nearly two decades of peaceful progressive leadership from President Compaore, if you don't count the two attempted coups followed by the speedy executions.

September 10: Arnold Palmer's Birthday

Although it can be said, as did Mark Twain, that "Golf is a good walk spoiled," it can be said as well that there is good in golf, in that it has resulted in so many fine quotations. It can be said that there is good in golf, in that it provides us with lines like "The difference between Tiger Woods at the Masters, and Princess Diana, is that Tiger had the better driver."

Golf reveals a man's true nature, as it has been said that "if there is larceny in any man, golf will bring it out." Arnold Palmer, whose birthday is today, once said, "I have a tip that can take five strokes off anyone's game. It's called an eraser." Which is just another way of saying, as did Paul Harvey, that "golf is a game in which one yells fore, shoots six, and writes down five." And H.L. Mencken wrote, "If I had my way, any man guilty of golf would be ineligible for any office of trust in the United States." It has been said that nothing has made more liars out of more Americans than golf; with the exception, said Will Rogers, of the income tax.

And it has also been said there are two things Americans voluntarily and eagerly purchase which are 100% guaranteed to make them feel angry and impotent: a computer and a golf club. 1958 U.S. Open winner Terrible Tommy Bolt, who would routinely throw tantrums and clubs during championship play, offered the following advice: "If you are going to throw a club, it is important to throw it ahead of you, down the fairway, so you don't waste additional energy going back to pick it up." Sam Snead also offered advice for those frustrated with their game when he said his advice would be to lay off for three weeks, then quit for good. Mental health experts agree that all who profess to love golf are in clinical denial, unable to face the brutal truth that they are trapped in an abusive relationship.

From golf has issued many parables, in their wisdom describing the inhuman condition that is golf. Like the one about Herbert, who hooked his shot off the first tee badly over the clubhouse roof and soon after a friend drives his golf cart up and shouts, "Didn't you see what happened to your ball off the first tee?" To which Herbert replies that he saw it hook over the clubhouse roof but lost sight of it, to which his friend told him it ricocheted off the windshield of a van which lost control and hit a school bus which overturned and burst into flames and kids were rushed to the hospital in serious condition, to which Herbert exclaimed, "Oh my God! I have to do something! What can I do?" To which his friend suggests he open his clubface a bit. One characteristic present in other sports which is absent in golf is braggadocio. There is little strutting and posturing because golf is a game in which the Heimlich can't save even a Greg Norman from choking, and which will throw a Gary Player off as easily as a Brahma Bull at the rodeo. It was Lee Trevino who said that when he's on the golf course and a big lightning storm comes up, he just holds up his one-iron because not even God can hit a one-iron.

Which is another illustration of how golf is one of the world's chief sources of fine quotations. And by way of proof, I offer this anecdote from my own family. My cousin is G. Stanley Koehler, who is an actual poet, and Stan tells the story about how, some years ago, he was playing golf with the great American poet John Ciardi, and at one point Ciardi's putt glided past the hole and kept on going right to the edge of the green, at which he pulled a literary allusion out of his bag. There is a poem by John Greenleaf Whittier, who wrote poetry in the era when all the big poets had three names---such as William Cullen Bryant and Henry Wadsworth Longfellow---which contains the lines: "of all sad words of tongue or pen, the saddest are these: "It might have been!" And so right on the spot, at that hole at the Chautauqua golf course, Ciardi, a better poet than a golfer, spoke these words: "The saddest words a tongue can say, are, putt again, you're still away," which was a takeoff on Whittier, only wittier.

October: By the Beard of Odin, Let's Toast Columbus Day

I see by the historical almanac that October 12 is the actual day upon which Columbus made landfall in the Bahamas, although there is no record of anyone, on that occasion, celebrating Columbus Day, probably because, in 1492, it fell on a Friday. But it got me to thinking and thanking our lucky stars that it was the voyages from the Spanish Main which seeded the fertile furrows of manifest destiny with transplants from Western Europe, rather than the frosty forests of Scandinavia. Because we can be grateful that, today, across this blessed nation, Vikings number only 56 players and 17 coaches, unless one counts the cheerleaders which is another 28, including two Kellys with a "Y" and one with an "I," because fate may well have made Vikings of us all.

History records this is also the week, scarcely a thousand years ago, that Leif Erikson, whose nickname was Leif the Lucky, landed on the shores of what is now New England after having visited Newfoundland. Sticklers for detail might credit with the discovery of the New World, Bjarni Herjolfsson, a Viking seaman who had been blown off course on an earlier voyage and reported seeing land to the west though he did not make a landfall. And these were Norsemen, as all Viking's were, although not all Norsemen were Vikings, in that stay-at-home Norsemen were just Norsemen, in what would become Norway, Sweden, and Denmark, and it was only the Norsemen who went Viking, which was the expression meaning adventuring or raiding or exploring, upon whom was bestowed the V-word.

And they were ferocious and ruthless warriors who raided the British Isles and the coast of Europe. And the Norman invasion of England was not, as many suppose, an invasion by Frenchmen but by Vikings, because the Normans derived their name from Norsemen who had seized territory in France which they named Normandy, and their duke in 1066 was known as William the Bastard who understandably preferred, "the Conqueror." And fortunate we are that the Norse discovery of the New World did not lead to our becoming a Viking nation and that Columbus sailed the ocean blue to claim the continent for a Christian God.

Not that the Norsemen were godless. On the contrary, had Norse culture proliferated through the new world, we would be fairly overrun with gods, and business meetings might adjourn with the oath, "By the sword of Odin, we will land the Baxter account!" Because whereas in Islam there is but one God and Allah be his name, and, in Christianity, deities number three, max, in the Trinity; in Norse theology there were two entire races of gods where Odin presided over the meetings of the Aesir in Asgard at the big conference table around which sat Balder, Bragi, Forsetti, Frigg, Heimdall, Idunn, Sif, Thor, Ull, Vali and Vidar, and the other race was the Vanir, who resided in Vanaheim, which is not home to the Angels in a suburb of Los Angeles but one of the nine worlds. After a war as part of the treaty, the Vanir sent hostages to Asgard including Frya, Freyr, and

Njord. Beneath these executive gods are scores of middle-management gods who were higher on the theological flow chart than frost giants, dwarves, ogres and elves, all of whom had special powers like the members of the Justice League.

Had Vikings overspread the New World their ferocity might have repelled the colonial powers and today our linguistic patois would include expressions such as, "By the beard of Balder I have forgotten my PIN number!" Or, "It is the mischief of Loki the trickster this Dr. Pepper machine refuses my dollar." It has been observed that the Norse creation stories, which would be the equivalent to the Christian Bible, read like a DragonQuest Dungeon Master's role-playing rulebook. We'd, all of us, employ far different exclamations and invectives. For example: "By the hammer of Thor, I have not accepted a package from a stranger nor allowed my bags out of my sight." "By Aurvandil's Toe, could this checkout line move any slower?" Or, "By the gods of Asgard, our defensive secondary is sucking out loud."

November 5: Roy Rogers' Birthday

Today is Roy Rogers' birthday. Or would be, were he not compost. And I happen to know that the first film appearance of Roy Roger's horse was in the Errol Flynn movie Robin Hood. Named Golden Cloud at that time, if you take a look at the horse Olivia De Havilland, as Maid Marion, is riding, you will see the future Trigger: "The Smartest Horse in Movies." And Roy Rogers was given Golden Cloud to ride in a movie and was so taken with it that he paid 25 hundred dollars to buy him in

1938, and his sidekick Smiley Burnett suggested changing the horse's name to Trigger.

And I know this, like I know that Dale Evan's horse was Buttermilk, which, along with Trigger and Bullet has marbles for eyes in a taxidermal diorama at the Double R-Bar in Roy's museum in Victorville, California, because all of us guys soon to pass out of the sunny side into the shade of fifty, wanted to be like Roy. The King of the Cowboys shot straight and played fair and always called a lady Ma'am, and took off his cowboy hat in their presence. And it was just natural that the King of the Cowboys would be married to the Queen of the West. And that he rode The Smartest Horse in Movies.

And we would sneer when John Wayne or Audie Murphy would gun down an outlaw on Main Street because clearly their shooting skills were so inferior as to be unable to shoot the weapon out of their adversary's hand like Roy always did. And after the day was won, Roy could holster his pearl-handled six-guns with three spins forward and three spins backward. And Roy could yodel without anybody making fun of him. And when he got shot we knew it would always be a flesh wound. And we all made lariats out of clotheslines and tried to twirl them so we could jump inside the spinning rope circle like Roy did, or lasso our younger brother or small domesticated animals. And Roy Rogers said howdy to strangers without them saying howdy first, and was always in a good mood. Other cowboys had a dark side; even Jimmy Stewart in *Bend of the River*, 1952, when he was delivering the supplies to the settlers and they were stolen by Arthur Kennedy and Harry Morgan. His homicidal rage simmered just beneath the surface. But Roy Rogers had no dark side, and lived by the code of the west, which was unwritten, but which we understood to mean, Be Nice, and When You Encounter Someone Who is Not Nice, Either pay Him No Mind or Shoot the Gun Out of His Hand. And from Roy, we learned to always drink upstream from the herd. And that a smile from a good woman is worth more'n a dozen from a bartender. And to never squat with your spurs on. And that it's easier to ride a horse in the direction it's goin'.

And I remember writing to Roy Rogers when I was around twelve that I thought he looked better in the neckerchief than the bolo tie, and he wrote back thanking me for my opinion. And it wasn't a surprise that Roy Rogers wrote me back, because, to young fans like me, the surprise would have been if he hadn't. Because he was Roy Rogers, King of the Cowboys. And even the more vulgar boys of my acquaintance admired Roy, even Glen Orcutt, who had the dirtiest mouth in the fourth grade, and told the one about how Roy Rogers and two other cowpokes were sitting around the fire after a day in the saddle and the first cowboy commenced to bragging about how tough he was and said, "I'm so tough that when I see a rattlesnake, I bite its head off and suck out the poison for a pick-me-up," and the second cowboy says, "Oh Yeah? Well, I'm so tough that when a grizzly attacked my cows, I whupped it with just one hand, slapped a saddle on it and used it as a horse for two years." Roy Rogers said nothing, simply staring into the fire and continuing to stir the coals with his penis." And I think you'll agree that Glen meant no disrespect.

December 25: Comet and Cupid and Dahmer and Nixon

I once wrote a treatise whose thesis was the human truths conveyed in the lyrics of secular Christmas songs such as Frosty the snowman and Rudolph the Red Nosed Reindeer. The parable of Frosty is analogous to the Phoenix legend of decay and rebirth, corporeal immortality reincarnate as a symbol for the continuum of life. It is also an affirmation of the "carpe diem" exhortation; the snowman's fatalistic philosophizing illustrated never so well as when, "Frosty the snowman, knew the sun was hot that day, So he said 'Let's run and have some fun, now, before I melt away." And the Rudolph myth evokes the classic redemptive-action-gains-acceptance-for-the-ugly-duckling fable, in which the protagonist (possessed of some disfigurement or handicap eliciting derision from his peers, as in the Quasimodo tale) performs a noble act, which apotheosizes and ennobles the now-accepted former outcast. Rudolph is an allegory for the ostracized; an allegory lost upon Bruce Manchester, whom, in the sixth grade, unfortunately discovered that "Had a very shiny nose" rhymed nicely with hose and blows. And what he did to "Oh Holy Night" is sure to be highlighted and underlined in the bouncer's notes at Heaven's gate.

We youthful blasphemers delighted in singing, "When shepherds washed their socks by night," and "Hark, the hairy angels sing." Which I recalled as I read about a school teacher in Everett, Massachusetts, who got himself into a Christmas pickle over alternative lyrics to the Rudolph song. This grade school teacher passed out printed lyrics for a song called, "Deadeye the Two-Gun Slinger," a portion of which goes, "Then one foggy Christmas Eve, Santa came to say, "Deadeye with your gun so bright, won't you shoot my wife tonight?" And of course when they heard about it the horrified mothers of the cherubs in this teacher's chorus of angels suffered palpitations and attacks of the vapors, and loudly called for the public evisceration of this monster corrupter of innocent youth. Parental opinion held that beloved childhood holiday folk melodies should be inviolate from alteration and abasing adulteration; failing to recollect the songs we all sang in elementary school, which were, in aggregate, quite twisted, because we were kids, and by nature mean and rotten.

I can never hear the "Battle Hymn of the Republic" without my lips mouthing the words, "Mine eyes have seen the glory of the burning of the school. We have tortured all the teachers and have broken all the rules. We are marching down the hall right now to kill the principal. Our gang is marching on," followed by the excellent chorus: "Glory, glory hallelujah! Teacher hit me with a ruler. I hid behind the door with a loaded .44, and she ain't my teacher anymore." Or the verse to "This Land is Your Land," that Woody Guthrie did not write, which goes, "This land is my land, It isn't your land. If you don't get off, I'll blow your head off. I got a shotgun, And you ain't got one. This land was made for only me." And Christmas parody songs are a grade school staple because they are so easy to make up. As an exercise, I thought one up today: "Oh I can't help but feel foreboding, As Instagram is loading, The baud rate is way down low, so Net is slow, Net is slow, Net is slow." Some of my contemporaries in second grade thought "We Three Kings of Orient Are, Two in a Taxi, One in a Car," was high comedy. But Stumo and Pads and I much preferred, "We Three Kings of Orient Are, Puffing on a giant cigar. It was loaded, it exploded"…and then in practiced unison we would go, "BLAM!" and pause two beats and conclude…Si…ii...lent Night. Which, granted, is sophomoric, but downright intellectual compared to the best my son Jonathan's generation could come up with. "Jingle Bells, Batman Smells, Robin laid an egg, The Batmobile lost a wheel, And the Joker got away, Hey!" Now that's just stupid.

Hang on. Just two more to go. A pair of Raves that actually didn't make the cut but they looked up at me with sad eyes and they are my children so what could I do?

April Schmay-pril

April is the official month in which to celebrate the poet, in case you didn't know it. April is National Poetry Month, as declared by The Academy of American Poets, an organization of Americans who presumably use the word, "Thanatopsis," more frequently than you do. And to commemorate this occasion, outgoing U.S. Poet Laureate Robert Pinsky announced the result of his two year expedition from the redwood forests to the Gulf Stream waters, to discover America's single favorite poem that does not begin, "There was a young girl from Purdue."

And out of the eighteen thousand poems he presented to the Library of Congress, far and away the most popular is "The Road Not Taken," by Robert Frost. The one where Mr. Frost cogitates for a while in deciding which road to take and winds up taking the one which appears less traveled by virtue of the grass being less worn, which goes to show how poets march to a different drummer—in that most of us would have taken the road leading to where we were going. And Mr. Stunkel in American Lit called it a metaphor for choices we make, and made us write in our notes that it was also an inducement, summoning us to individuality; to depart the herd and take the less trammeled path to self-realization born of nonconformity. Which, ironically, he expected us all to express in exactly those words in the blue book test.

And April being declared American Poetry Month by American poets is illustrative of the narcissism lurking in the genes of all poets, who, more than anything, love writing poems about themselves and each other. Such as John Crowe Ransom who wrote, "I dip my hat to Chaucer, Swilling soup from his saucer. And to Master Shakespeare, who wrote big on small beer. The abstemious Wordsworth, subsisted on a curd's-worth. But a slick one was Tennyson, putting gravy on his venison. What these men had to eat and drink, is what we say and what we think. The influence of Milton came wry out of Stilton. Sing a song for Percy Shelley, drowned in pale lemon jelly. And for precious Keats, Dripping blood of pickled beets. Then there was poor

Willie Blake, He foundered on sweet cake. God have mercy on the sinner, who must write with no dinner. No gravy and no grub, no pewter and no pub. No belly and no bowels, only consonants and vowels." Which wears a bit thin, because although I'll give him Wordsworth and curd's-worth, it doesn't take a bonded-licensed poet to rhyme Keats and beets.

And there was James Russell Lowell, who, in 1848, slammed fellow poet Edgar Allen Poe, thusly: "There comes Poe with his raven, like Barnaby Rudge, Three fifths of him genius and two fifths, sheer fudge. Who talks like a book of iambs and pentameters, In a way to make people of common sense damn metres."

Of American poetry, American poet Louise Simpson wrote, "Whatever it is, it must have A stomach that can digest Rubber, coal, uranium, moons, poems. Like the shark, it contains a shoe, It must swim for miles through the desert, Uttering cries that are almost human." A thought doubtless regarded as deep by those with the luxury of time to squander thinking about it, but which would have been retained in our memories far longer had she gone the extra mile to rhyme something with uranium. Perhaps inside the shark there could have been a cranium. Or a geranium.

Anyhow, American poetry did injury to my grade point average when I disagreed with Mr. Stunkel's interpretation of "The Road not Taken" as indicative of America's free-thinking rugged individualism. Instead, rather than individualistic in the extreme, it can be argued, as in the verse by Malvina Reynolds, that ours is a conformist culture which lives in: "little boxes, made of ticky-tacky, little boxes on the hillside, little boxes, all the same." And it happens that this is the centennial anniversary of the birth of folk poet Malvina Reynolds, which is an occasion worthy of the crafting of an "Ode to Malvina," which I am glad not to involve myself in, since collecting words to rhyme with Malvina will be dicey at best. Anyhow, we are far more likely to blow past the road less traveled fifteen miles over the speed limit because the lights would slow us down and Dawson's Creek is on at seven. In our mythology, we are independent free-spirited Huck Finns. In practice, our rhino bars are all for show and we don't do intellectual off-roading. As a nation indivisible, we are not by nature individualistic, which is illustrated by how, on the way to choosing a national poem, "The Road Not Taken" was, with poetical paradox, the road most taken.

Hot Time in the Big City

I was at the health club this morning in an effort to deal with the destructive aftermath of five weeks of red and green M&Ms, and, in that an idea for today's Rave had not, up to that moment, made itself known to me, I entered the Men's locker room sauna with the intention of conjuring a topic for today, and was engrossed in contemplation when the Naked Placemat Man from Idaho arrived. I know this because he told me, right after commenting on the weather and allowing as how this was the biggest gymnasium he'd ever seen in his life. And he asked me how many floors it was and I said counting the pool on the roof, seven, and he said "Dang," an interjection which derailed my train of thought and did injury to my reverie, as I subscribe to the opinion of Henry David Thoreau, who said, "I never found a companion that was so companionable as solitude."

And when it became clear that this visitor to our city from the American west was delighted to have found a native with whom to palaver, I briefly thought to remove myself to the steam room and its deafening pressure valve, hissing so as to prohibit conversation. But in the steam room lurks the potential for the acquisition of the numberless viruses and bacterial respiratory infections shared by the diseased breaths of fellow club members; the toxic germs adhering to the suspended molecules, awaiting the opportunity to be inhaled by a currently healthy me. So in the sauna I remained, as the Naked Idaho Placemat Man blessedly covered his lap with a towel and explained that he was in Chicago for a week to attend the International Housewares Show, and he is going to see the sights for a few days before setting up the booth, at which he will sell placemats. And he's peddled placemats for eight years, since he bought out a veteran mat man who was moving to Alamogordo to be with his daughter, and that he got the inspiration for his new idea from watching cable TV, when it occurred to him that the TV screen had nigh onto the same dimensions as a placemat. And all the channels have their logo in the lower right-hand corner, and so he figured to offer vinyl placemats with the customer's logo or design in the lower corner, and vinyl is best because, on vinyl, scenic photographs fairly jump off the mat, clarity-wise. And I might have inquired as to the identities of those whom he envisioned clamoring for the opportunity to dine from these vinyl-scenic-logo placemats, had I an infinitesimal impulse to speak aloud, which I did not, in agreement, as I am, with whomever said "Solitude is the triumph of mind over chatter."

And it was around about this point that another stranger entered the sauna, and stood for a moment, before expressing the opinion that it was too hot. Which seemed a peculiar thing to say because he was in a sauna. As in the expression on a day in August when someone is sure to say, "Wow, it's a sauna outside today." A sauna is the definition of hot. One expects a sauna to be hot enough to cause one to lose a pound of water-weight in twenty minutes expending zero effort. Hot enough to poach sea bass. But happily, Mr. Naked Idaho Placemat took Mr. Too Hot's comment as an invitation to dialogue, releasing me from the obligation of having to summon up some pleasantry pertaining to Idaho, of which I know nothing, aside from that its Russets were on sale at Dominick's on Sunday for 79 cents for a ten pound bag, a bargain which occurs three times a year, tops. Too soon, Mr. Too Hot departed, on the grounds that it was too hot.

And I hoped the resulting silence would be sustained, undamaged, because a sauna is a chapel of quiet contemplation, like a Navajo sweat lodge; a place for inward communion with the spirit; an inappropriate forum for a monologue by a placemat-printing pilgrim performing his Haj to the Mecca of housewares. As he resumed his soliloquy to observe that the winter in Pocatello has been relatively mild, I concentrated the power of my mind on the thermostat to up the heat so as to drive him away and allow me to exercise my inalienable right to solitude, which Supreme Court Justice Louis Brandeis called, "The most comprehensive of rights, and the right most valued by civilized men."

Sadly, focusing all my mental powers failed to drive the temperature above 178, still 34 degrees short of that required to cook him through like a littleneck clam in a steamer. It was when he boasted how his hotel had a phone and a TV in the bathroom, right by the toilet, that I exited, as I wished to be absent before the Naked Idaho Placemat Man busted out with, "Everything's up to date in Kansas City, they've gone about as fur as they kin go."

This is the end of the book. If you read these words, please know that I admire your endurance and appreciate you squandering the time. To hear more monologues spoken aloud and other entertainments, I invite you to visit www.davemcbride.com .

About the Author

Dave McBride is a broadcast journalist who, for more than twenty years, wrote and performed radio humor essays daily for the amusement of Chicago radio listeners. Dave is a winner of an Edward R. Murrow Award for Best Large Market Writing for Radio and the Best Radio Writing World Gold Medal by the New York Festivals International media awards. After decades of work as a broadcast journalist Dave has traded frigid Midwest Februarys in the big city for the Gulf Stream breezes rustling through the palms in sub-tropical South Florida.

By Dave McBride
Lock, Stock & Peril—A Milo Bird Mystery
The Book of Raves—An Anthology

Find more at www.davemcbride.com

www.ingramcontent.com/pod-product-compliance
Lightning Source LLC
Chambersburg PA
CBHW051751040426
42446CB00007B/309